CATCH THE FIRE!!!

CATCH the *fire*!!!

A Cross-Generational Anthology of Contemporary African-American Poetry

Edited by Derrick I. M. Gilbert (a.k.a. D-Knowledge)
With the special editorial direction of Tony Medina

RIVERHEAD BOOKS, NEW YORK

Riverhead Books
Published by The Berkley Publishing Group
A member of Penguin Putnam Inc.
200 Madison Avenue
New York, New York 10016

First edition: February 1998

The Putnam Berkley World Wide Web site address is
http://www.berkley.com

Library of Congress Cataloging-in-Publication Data
Catch the fire!!! : a cross-generational anthology of contemporary
   African-American poetry / edited by Derrick I. M. Gilbert (a.k.a.
   D-Knowledge) with the special editorial direction of Tony Medina.—
   1st ed.
      p.   cm.
   ISBN 1-57322-654-8 (acid-free paper)
   1. American poetry—Afro-American authors.   2. American
poetry—20th century.   3. Afro-Americans—Poetry.   I. Gilbert,
Derrick I. M.   II. Medina, Tony.
PS591.N4C35   1998
811'.5080896073—dc21   97-30173

Printed in the United States of America

10   9   8   7   6   5   4   3

CONTENTS

Acknowledgments   xi

Introduction   xiii

Chapter 1 **What's Going On?**

Interview with June Jordan   3

AMIRI BARAKA, "Of What Use Is Poetry? (Babalu Meets the Wolfman)"   8

KENNETH CARROLL, "The Domino Theory (Or Snoop Dogg Rules the World)"   8

KEITH ANTAR MASON, "Friday Night"   11

PAM WARD, "She Should Have Called 911"   13

VICTOR E. BLUE, "American Dialogue"   15

DR. MADD VIBE (A.K.A. THE MISSIN' LINK), "L.A. (Lost Assholes)"   16

KALUNDA-RAE, "Hoochie Route"   16

NIKKIA BILLINGSLEY, "Rhetorically Speaking"   19

ELAINE BROWN, "If Randi Could Write"   20

LETTA SIMONE-NEFERTARI NEELY, "Rhonda, Age 15 Emergency Room"   25

ASHA BANDELE, "the subtle art of breathing"   32

KEVIN POWELL, "Out of Pocket"   36

CHARLIE R. BRAXTON, "The Gathering"   41

CHRISTOPHER STANARD, "Spirits Struggle"   42

EL RIVERA, "Elegy for a Martyred Poet"   43

KAMAU DAÁOOD, "Tears"   43

BILL DUKE, "Poem to the World"   46

DERRICK I. M. GILBERT (A.K.A. D-KNOWLEDGE), "Too Many"   48

JUNE JORDAN, "Poem for Derrick Gilbert"   51

Chapter 2 **It's a Family Affair**

Interview with Amiri Baraka   57

AMIRI BARAKA, "Revolutionary Love"   62

TOI DERRICOTTE, "Christmas Eve: My Mother Dressing"   63

EVELYN E. SHOCKLEY, "Oseola McCarty"   64

ROHAN B. PRESTON, "Lovesong to My Father"   67

PAULA WHITE-JACKSON, "Saturday Morning Pancakes"   68

BEVERLY FIELDS BURNETTE, "Artichoke Pickle Passion: Sonnet"   69

RONI WALTER, "Familee Reunion Tyme"   69

NIAMA LESLIE WILLIAMS, "Companion Pieces"   71

MERILENE M. MURPHY, "Fat Grass & Slow Rain"   73

LENARD D. MOORE, "Tanka"   77

LENARD D. MOORE, "Haiku"   77

LYNN G. MOORE, "Haiku"   77

MAIISHA L. MOORE, "Haiku"   78

BRIAN GILMORE, "Hazing"   78

MAWIYAH KAI EL-JAMAH BOMANI, "Homecoming"   79

E. ETHELBERT MILLER, "Mountain Wife"   80

M. ELIZA HAMILTON, "Things I Do Not Speak"   81

SHAQUILLE O'NEAL, "Biological Didn't Bother"   83

NADIR LASANA BOMANI, "Thin Water"   87

V. KALI NURIGAN, "I'm Raising Children"   88

HAKI R. MADHUBUTI, "A Bonding"   90

Chapter 3 **No Ordinary Love**

Interview with Ntozake Shange   95

NTOZAKE SHANGE, "The Lizard Series"   98

SABAH AS-SABAH, "Love"   102

K. CURTIS LYLE, "Your Tears Feel Good on the Hood of My Car"   103

JAMAL, "Sat. Nite"   106

WENDY L. JAMES, "Troy"   107

A. K. TONEY, "In the Twilight"   108

JENOYNE ADAMS, "Out-of-Body Experience"   109

DJ RENEGADE, "Hoodoo"   111

ANTHONY C. LYONS, "Touch Her"   112

SHONDA BUCHANAN, "Prayer"   114

MICHAEL DATCHER, "i am open"   115

KUPENDA AUSET (JOETTE HARLAND WATTS), "That Was
   Then"   123

DERRICK X (A.K.A. GOLDIE THE POET), "Shot to the Curb"   125

CHERYL BOYCE TAYLOR, "English Lace"   126

DURIEL E. HARRIS, "But There Are Miles"   127

KYSHA N. BROWN, "Brown Girl Blues"   128

HONORÉE F. JEFFERS, "I Was Looking at Miles"   131

CREE SUMMER, "Curious White Boy"   132

MALCOLM-JAMAL WARNER, "My Woman"   133

GLENN JOSHUA, "On the Morning St. Bernard"   134

LISA B. THOMPSON, "What Do I Want from Men and
   Love?"   136

LANA MOORER (A.K.A. MC LYTE), "Everyday"   139

OJENKE, "Amazon"   141

Chapter 4 **Revolutions**

Interview with Abiodun Oyewole   145

ABIODUN OYEWOLE, "When the Revolution Comes"   149

MARIO VAN PEEBLES, "To Hell with Whitey"   150

CHUCK D, "But Can You Kill the Nigga in You?"   152

ROLAND POET X, "The Divided States of America"   154

SPEECH, "Revolution"   157

OKTAVI, "Pardon Me"   159

POETRI, "Don't Hate Me!"   161

TONY MEDINA, "Capitalism Is a Brutal Motherfucker"   162

NADIR LASANA BOMANI, "A Philosophical Perspective on
   Everyday Shit"   168

EDDIE GRIFFIN, "Mind of a Madman"   168

ADWIN BROWN, "Donut Man"   169

CRYSTAL A. WILLIAMS, "In Search of Aunt Jemima"   170

TA-NEHISI COATES, "Alice Flips the Script"   173

A(E)RIN WILSON, "Grenudita"   174

PAUL CALDERÓN, "It's Hard!"   177

JOHN W. LOVE, JR., "Moment 9/The Woman"   181

MARIAHADESSA "EKERE" TALLIE, "Karma's Footsteps"   183

ABIODUN OYEWOLE, "Future Shock"   185

Chapter 5 Body & Soul/Celebrations

Interview with Quincy Troupe   191

DJ RENEGADE, "Haiku"   196

MICHAEL WAR, "Duke Checks Out Ella As She Scats Like That"   197

ART NIXON, "Ju-Ju Man"   199

ASKIA M. TOURÉ, "Milestones: September 28, 1991"   202

MENDI LEWIS, "I Remember 1983"   203

DEFARI HERUT, "Gems"   204

MARLON C. WILLIAMS (POETX), "Blood, Sweat, and Fears"   205

T'KALLA, "Nuns in the Basement of God"   206

CHEZIA THOMPSON-CAGER, "Praise Song for Katherine Dunham: A Choreopoem"   208

CANDICE M. JENKINS, "Poem for Tracy (Chapman)"   210

LANA C. WILLIAMS, "Flying High"   212

KAREN WILLIAMS, "Kissing Keys"   213

PATRICIA SMITH, "Asking for a Heart Attack"   214

QUINCY TROUPE, "Collage"   216

Chapter 6 Catch the Fire

Interview with Sonia Sanchez   221

SONIA SANCHEZ, "Catch the Fire"   225

KALAMU YA SALAAM, "Soon One Morning, I'll Fly Away"   227

JERRY W. WARD, JR., "At the Border of Constant Disaster"   228

ANGELA SHANNON, "Doris"   229

DERRICK I. M. GILBERT (A.K.A. D-KNOWLEDGE), "Miracle"   230

GLENIS REDMOND SHERER, "Our Spirit Stands"   233

JABARI ASIM, "Mumble the Magic Words"   234

KWAME ALEXANDER, "Just Us"   235

ERIC PRIESTLEY, "Eye & Eye"   236

SAUL WILLIAMS, "Recitation"   237

SONJA MARIE, "Dream Fix"   238

SABAH AS-SABAH, "Sister Roll"   240

YONA HARVEY, "Sonia Told the Women"   241

DERRICK I. M. GILBERT (A.K.A. D-KNOWLEDGE), "The Fire in the Drum"   243

PETER J. HARRIS, "Let's All Take the Blame"   246

AMIRI BARAKA, "Revelation in Brick City"   249

HAILE GERIMA, "Sankofa"   250

NIKKI GIOVANNI, "But Since You Finally Asked"   252

Contributors   255

Credits   281

Index of Contributors   287

ACKNOWLEDGMENTS

Tony Medina: Thank you. Thank you. Thank you. This anthology would not exist without you. This anthology is you—for you are the fire.

Ramon Hervey: You are so much more than my *manager*—for you are my steadfast friend. You mean more to me than a paper acknowledgment could ever express.

Cindy Spiegel: It was often tedious, but you always made the process worthwhile and actually enjoyable. You are a great editor and a gracious spirit.

Matt Bialer: Thanks for making an idea a reality.

June Jordan, Amiri Baraka, Ntozake Shange, Abidoun Oyewole, Quincy Troupe, and Sonia Sanchez: Thank you for your support, guidance, and love.

Michael Datcher, E. Ethelbert Miller, Rohan B. Preston, Lenard D. Moore, Kalamu Ya Salaam, and Charlie R. Braxton: Thanks for connecting me with so many wonderful poets, and for being patient with me. Collectively, you are my personified Web site.

And thank you to all the contributors, and to all the poets of the world. I am because we are and because we are therefore I am.

Finally, this book is dedicated to the most exquisitely poetic woman I know—my mom.

In 1993 a friend of mine named Michael Datcher invited me to a poetry reading he was coordinating. But the idea of attending a poetry reading was not remotely appealing to me. After all, I envisioned walking into a dark, candlelit room with featherweight incense sparring with my eyes and nose. I thought the inhabitants would be postmodern Bippies (that is, Black hippies) who snapped their fingers, or snapped their toes, or snapped their earlobes as a means of expressing themselves. As for their poetry . . . well, I expected these Bippies to read poems that were deliberately aloof, forcefully abstract, redundantly elusive, and just universally nonsensical. Rather than attend a poetry reading, I would have preferred staying home—perhaps scrubbing toilets or clipping my fingernails.

Michael was a persistent brotha, though. Even after several months of my contriving clever excuses, he continued to ask me when I was going to check out what he referred to as "the Anansi Writers' Workshop." Finally, one Wednesday afternoon Michael appealed to my carnality: "Hey, D . . . there's some beautiful sistahs who've been coming to the workshop!" My external and internal response was a prolonged "hmmmmm." When I mentally finished the inflection on my last *m*, I found myself driving to attend the so-called workshop.

The Anansi Writers' Workshop was held at a small venue owned by legendary jazz drummer Billy Higgins, located at The World Stage in an area of Los Angeles known as Leimert Park. As I entered the small white building I abruptly thought: "This don't *look* that bad." After all, the thirty (or so) folks occupying the space looked quite normal—albeit I identified a few potential avant-garde, bohemian Bippie types. The small room was well lit, though there were a few incense sticks burning. But this incense did not smell a quarter bad; in fact, I was not even upset when a six-foot five-inch brotha stood on a chair and pulled a long string that propelled a ceiling fan—

which inevitably expanded the boundaries of the frankincented fumes. And, oh yeah, being a wannabe mack at the time—one who had been reeled into a poetry reading with some "playa bait"—I quickly observed that there were indeed some beautiful sistahs at the stage. Hmm . . .

Once I got beyond the aesthetics, I sat down and prepared myself to listen to the poetry. "Here comes the torture," I thought to myself. However, my stereotypes about poetry and poets were swiftly and skillfully assassinated by a bevy of young, old, and middle-aged wordsmiths. As we say in the neighborhood, "I couldn't even front." I mean these poets were talking about real stuff—love, hate, drugs, R&B, vengeance, forgiveness, rap, rape, racism, capitalism, sexism, eroticism, and a bunch of other "isms." Rhythmic energy flung itself around the room faster and more gracefully than the air propelled by the ceiling fan. The small room began feeling like an uncharted universe with an awe-inspiring constellation of poets. This poetry reading was like a religious revival, and I was being saved. Can I get a witness?

I cannot recall what happened in my life the following six days, twenty-three hours, and fifty-nine minutes, but I do know that at precisely 7:30 P.M. the following Wednesday I was back at the Anansi Workshop. Again, I was mesmerized and felt the urge to speak in poetic tongues. I wondered: "Has a poetry spell been cast on me?" Then another week sprinted by, and I was back at the workshop. However, this time I was armed with a single-caliber poem crumpled in my back pocket. And bang . . . my overloaded words ricocheted in my gut as I shared my newly discovered poetic voice. And the congregation said "Amen."

Within a month I became an Anansi zealot. My first task was to write and perform as much poetry as was physically and metaphysically possible. Shortly thereafter, I embarked on a poetry mission. I began reciting at venues throughout Los Angeles . . . then throughout California . . . then on concert stages across the States . . . then on national television shows . . . then in motion pictures . . . then for Quincy Jones's record label . . . and even on a Rolling Stones' CD-ROM.

Although I was constantly refining my poetry performance (or my "spoken word"), I was not committing the same fervor to my written words/to my feelings/to my craft. Unfortunately, I often see many young poets spinning horizontally into this abyss—particularly given the commercialization of poetry through such media as television, film, CDs, and emerging interactive technologies. And, of course, poets should flow with change; however, poets should always cultivate their craft—which is what I was neglecting to do. My poetry was impersonal, banal, repetitive, superficial, and full of clichés. Sometimes I would actually review my poems and ask myself: "Who wrote this bleep/bleep?" I was doing poetry for performance's sake; I was a passionless poetry zombie.

Then one evening the filmmaker John Singleton and I went to hear Sonia Sanchez recite her poetry at Eso Won Bookstore in Los Angeles. Hearing Sonia brought back feelings from my first experience at the Anansi Writers' Workshop. After her reading, she was asked what advice she would give young poets. She responded by saying that poets should always study and hone their craft. But the most memorable thing she said was: "Read, read . . . and when you are done reading, read some more." After her presentation, John and I introduced ourselves and had a brief conversation with her. I do not recall the specifics of the conversation, but I do remember picking Sonia up from her hotel the next morning and taking her to Leimert Park. Almost instantaneously, Sonia became my mentor, my guide, and my friend. In fact, Sonia's words—and her example—inspired me to familiarize myself with the works of other poets.

Even before I became active in the poetry scene, I was a voracious reader; however, most of what I read was social-scientific, theoretical, and historical texts. As I began my immersion into *poetry* I was not compelled to study poets from the Western canon (e.g., Whitman, Frost, Browning, Dickinson, Blake, Longfellow, cummings, Wordsworth, Eliot, Pound, Tennyson, Pope, Shakespeare, et al). At that moment I was not even intrigued by African or so-called Third World poets. Nope! I wanted to read the poetry of Black folks right here in America. I began with the poetry of eighteenth- and nineteenth-century poets such as Phillis Wheatley, Jupiter Hammon, James Whitfield, Frances Watkins Harper, George Moses, and perhaps my favorite of that broadly defined period, Paul Laurence Dunbar. All of these writers taught me that freedom encompasses much more than just shedding shackles. I next found myself in the Harlem Renaissance—a period I had heard about, but had not become intimate with. As my literary gaze focused on the 1920s and 1930s, I was inspired and enchanted by the likes of James Weldon Johnson, Claude McKay, Georgia Douglas Johnson, Jean Toomer, Sterling Brown, Anne Spencer, Arna Bontemps, Countee Cullen, Angelina Grimké, and the ridiculously prolific, profluent, and profound Langston Hughes. After partying with these lindy hoppers of words, I acquainted myself with Gwendolyn Brooks and Margaret Walker. At this point the festive vibe ended—for I was infuriated that I had never read their work before, but that I was knowledgeable about nonBlack writers of the same period. I realized that I was living on a plantation of miseducation—picking cotton candy and bowing down to an invisible, yet omnipotent, master of ignorance. But, now, I was escaping.

I's gonna be free!!!!!!!!!

When I stopped running, I no longer saw slap-me-down clothing or conks or fashions from the 1920s. Instead, I saw a new Black Aesthetic—for I was experiencing the Black Arts movement. As an undergraduate at UC-Berkeley, I had submerged myself in the history of the Black Power movement. In doing so, I had become familiar with the names of poets who were directly or indirectly associated with the movement; actually, I had even read some of their work. However, as a sociology and rhetoric major who was being intellectually guided by Dr. Harry Edwards (a scholar and activist who figured prominently during the black power movement), I spent much of my time learning about such mythical figures as Stokely Carmichael, Huey Newton, Angela Davis, Maulana Karenga, Elaine Brown, H. Rap Brown, and—the guru of my fascination—Malcolm X. But now I was learning about, reading the works of, and—in some cases—listening to the recorded voices of such poets as Amiri Baraka, Jayne Cortez, Quincy Troupe, Nikki Giovanni, Carolyn Rodgers, Haki Madhubuti, Etheridge Knight, Mari Evans, The Last Poets, The Watts Prophets, and of course, Sonia Sanchez. I was captivated by their passion, their fury, their intensity, their candor, their rage, their flare, and their *fire*. My sojourn was not complete, as it will never be, but I was finally scorching. The zombie in me burned at an ancestrally rooted stake, and I was reborn again. Hallelujah!

As I continued reading the works of other poets, as I continued developing my craft, and as I continued interacting with other practitioners of the word, I began to understand experientially and viscerally the delectable tradition of Black/African-American poetry. I also observed poets from all generations, from various geographical locales, and from disparate backgrounds contributing to the maintenance of this tradition. In some places, poetry was even becoming trendy. And, by the mid-1990s, some folks were even talking about a "New Black Renaissance." But I refrained from labeling what I saw as a renaissance; instead, I saw it, and still see it, as a continuum of centuries of tradition. *Catch the Fire!!!* attempts to show the complexity of this continuum and the power of the African-American poetry tradition.

This anthology is born out of an emotional day I spent reciting poetry at one of Los Angeles' juvenile-corrections facilities. Many of the incarcerated boys and girls I met there were serving time for such crimes as armed robbery, arson, rape, and even premeditated murder. Although these adolescents enjoyed my poetry, I could see nihilism reflecting in their eyes. One caramel-complected, lanky teen with piercing black eyes and a four-inch jagged scar tearing down his right cheek even told me:

> Your words are dope, but muthufuckas just tryin' to survive up in here. . . . Dem poems can't stop a muthufucka from bein' offed and shit. But I likes ya flow.

Although I appreciated this young brotha's compliment, and although I was aware of the ubiquitous street survival ethos, I was still pained to hear this fifteen-year-old boy—with an eleven-year-old's body and voice—describe the situation so matter-of-factly. That day I saw hundreds of detained youth who were physically and mentally in bondage, but this boy became my image of the hopelessness and rage among primarily black and brown youth.

Later that evening I reread Sonia Sanchez's book *Wounded in the House of a Friend,* and I found myself fixated on her poem "Catch the Fire." Although I was familiar with this poem (as Sonia and I had recorded the piece for my poetry album, *All That and a Bag of Words*), it now had a new effect on me. After spending a spiritually draining day at juvenile hall, one passage reverberated in my consciousness:

> CATCH YOUR FIRE......... DON'T KILL
> HOLD YOUR FIRE.......... DON'T KILL
> LEARN YOUR FIRE......... DON'T KILL
> BE THE FIRE................ DON'T KILL

These words were like a soothing balm, assuaging my pessimism and ultimately giving me assurance that better days are coming real soon.

As her words healed me I recalled Sonia telling me how she came to write the poem. She had just had a conversation with Bill Cosby, in which they were discussing "what is going on" with Black children. The two agreed that this generation is faced with intense obstacles that are specific to the historical moment; they also saw that too many youth are stumbling in their attempts to overcome these barriers. These two legends were discussing what I had seen in juvenile hall—the hopelessness and the despair. This prompted Cosby to ask

Sonia: "Where's the fire . . . where's the passion with our youth?" Of course, the question was rhetorical, as both Cosby and Sonia knew the fire existed; the problem, as they collectively saw it, was that our youth are not tapping into it. Reflecting on this conversation, Sonia immediately wrote a revolutionary poem in which she encourages young brothas and sistahs to:

> catch the fire . . . and live
> > live.
> > livelivelivelive.
> > livelivelivelive.
> > live.
> > live.

And there it was: "Catch the Fire." This was the concept I was searching for to describe how I felt about the current wave of poetry. "Catch the Fire" was also apropos for describing those African-American poets who are continuing the tradition I had come to cherish. I realized then that I wanted to assemble a collection of poets so that others could catch the fire—so that readers could experience what I felt that first night at the Anansi Writers' Workshop.

Although all the poets represented in this anthology are torch carriers, some are poetic harbingers who have influenced multitudes. In fact, these celebrated poets have inspired most of the younger contributors in *Catch the Fire!!!*. Thus, at the beginning of each chapter, I have included interviews with June Jordan, Amiri Baraka, Ntozake Shange, Abiodun Oyewole, Quincy Troupe, and Sonia Sanchez. In these interviews, these cultural heroes and sheroes reflect on their lives within poetry, they comment on the poetry of now, and they also offer words of encouragement and direction for those who are dedicating themselves to the craft of words. These interviews are a symbolic passing of the fire—from established poets to emerging ones.

While reflecting on the tradition of African-American poetry, and after interviewing the poetry icons referred to above, I recognized that there were recurring topics that African-American poets were addressing. In *Catch the Fire!!!* I use song and poem titles as a way of broadly labeling these themes. Thus, Chapter 1 is entitled "What's Going On?"—inspired by Marvin Gaye's masterpiece song and album of the same title. The poems in this chapter express some of the many issues and themes that African-American poets are confronting. Poems in this chapter deal with subject matter ranging from street violence to sexual abuse to church burnings to hip-hop culture. This chapter begins with an interview with June Jordan, who challenges poets to assert a value system about "what should be going on." Jordan emphasizes that poets can actually produce work that helps instigate change, rather than eloquently recapitulating the problems.

What's in Chapter 2? Well . . . as Sly Stone would croon: "It's a Family Affair." Poems in this chapter reflect the beauty, the complexity, the diversity, the strength, and the resiliency of African-American families. Poems in this chapter speak of mothers, fathers, brothers, sisters, cousins, grandmothers, grandfathers, and other kinfolk. These poems also comment on extended notions of family—like your "peeps" or your "hommies." This chapter begins with an interview that Tony Medina and I conducted with Amiri Baraka. Although Baraka discusses a cross section of subjects in this interview, he prefaces his comments by suggesting that writing about family is essential because family is the foundation for establishing who we are.

What poetry anthology would be complete without a chapter of love poems? Not this one! But this ain't "No Ordinary Love" poem chapter. The poems in Chapter 3 deal with the complexity and perplexity of love. These poems range from the romantic to the erotic, from the irascible to the reconcilable, and from the hypnotic to the neurotic. This chapter begins with an interview with Ntozake Shange, who puts forth the powerful proclamation that "all poetry is love poetry."

Chapter 4 is somewhat deceptive. Initially, this chapter was entitled "When the Revolution Comes," inspired by The Last Poets' poem of the same title. I intended to offer poems that evoked issues of political, economic, and social revolutions. But as I began compiling poems for this chapter, I observed that many poets were dealing with personal revolutions. Some examples of these revolutions were bi/multiracial identity, womanhood, manhood, "coming-outhood" and various other introspective issues that some might popularly refer to as "identity politics." Consequently, I changed the title of this chapter to "Revolutions" in order to encompass all dimensions of the revolutionary construct. The "Revolution" chapter begins with an interview with Abiodun Oyewole of The Last Poets. Oyewole ultimately suggests that revolution, in whatever form, is fundamentally about evolution, growth, and change.

Chapter 5, "Body & Soul—Celebrations," presents a collage of poems that address various Black cultural expressions such as dance, music, sport, and other activities that emphasize our bodies and our souls. This chapter is cotitled "Celebrations" because many of the poems focus on individuals who exquisitely personify the concept of "Body & Soul." The chapter begins with an interview with Quincy Troupe, who submits that poetry should be anchored in an ocean of celebration.

Riding on the flames ignited by Sonia Sanchez's "Catch the Fire," the poems in this last chapter are inspirational, motivational, and uplifting. Not only do these poems emphasize catching the fire, they also encourage others to throw the fire . . . spread the fire . . . and— as Sonia says—"be the fire." This chapter begins with an interview with Sonia, who suggests that poetry is the greatest genre on earth and that we should always nurture it.

It is my hope that *Catch the Fire!!!* will provide readers with a reservoir of kerosene and a life supply of matches to ignite flames of tradition. I also hope this anthology excites others to become poetic pyromaniacs. But *Catch the Fire!!!* is not the beginning, middle, or end of African-American poetry; it is simply part of the constantly flowing continuum. Accordingly, I encourage people to read and collect other anthologies—such as LeRoi Jones (Amiri Baraka) and

Larry Neal's *Black Fire: An Anthology of Afro-American Writing*.* I cite this anthology because of its personal effect on me and because of its connection, in title and spirit, with this anthology. But I also hope that people collect the numerous other anthologies of African-American poetry—historical and contemporary. And I anticipate the publication of many more anthologies, as well as individual volumes of poetry—for I submit that multitudes will catch the fire . . . and live.

One final note regarding this anthology. Those familiar with African-American poets will observe noticeable voids—such as Gwendolyn Brooks, Maya Angelou, Ishmael Reed, Rita Dove, Yusef Komunyakaa, Margaret Walker, and a rainbow of others. In fact, several younger poets whom I know and respect—such as Ruth Forman, Reggie Gaines, and Ras Baraka (to name a few)—are not present in this book. But even though their works, and the works of many other gifted poets, are not included here, their spirit keeps this book burning. Conversely, some individuals present in this volume are not known for being poets—as I wanted to show that the fire is contagious and that diverse beings keep the flames maintained. Thus, included are poems from actors, actresses, lawyers, comedians, computer consultants, government workers, unemployed persons, and even an NBA all-star. I also wanted to show the broad parameters of a potentially limiting label—African-American poetry. To this end, I have included some rap lyrics—for, contrary to conventional absurdity, rap lyrics are poetry and rap is part of the African-American poetry continuum.

As we enter the new millennium we need to embrace life and hope. If not for our own sake, for our children's sake. *Catch the Fire!!!* is dedicated to the youth, but it is inspired by all those who have dedicated their lives to positive poetic change—whether they are poets or not. Despite media coverage, there is so much to look forward to; and this anthology is but an eye blink of what is to come.

*Unfortunately, this volume is out of print and is only available at some libraries. I thus encourage *someone* to reprint this important collection.

Catch the Fire!!! stands on the pillars of optimism, not nihilism or despair. *Catch the Fire!!!* is fueled by love, not anger or malevolence. *Catch the Fire* exists because there is a burning tradition . . . because there is heated talent and simmering dedication . . . and because there is FIRE. *Burn, baby, burn!!!*

CATCH THE FIRE!!!

chapter 1

What's Going On?

INTERVIEW

Derrick Gilbert What do you think is the role of the poet/writer/artist as we approach the end of the twentieth century?

June Jordan I think the artist has the responsibility to produce work that's true and helpful out here. I think that all of us are staggering right now from a tremendous amount of disinformation and distracting materials—materials that distract us from "what's goin' on" and what needs to be taken care of. You can see, for example, in the clobbering of the so-called Black welfare queens precisely what I'm talking about. I hoped that there would have been a huge coming together of artists/filmmakers/dancers/musicians/poets to stop this nonsense—to say this is not true, this is not right. Poets and other artists need to play a role in the prevention of the humiliation that is inflicted upon those who rely on the welfare program. And that's just one example.

Secondly, there's the need for the artist, in whatever medium, to assert a value system that says: "This is what I believe is good and necessary . . . and most important." Do that as persuasively as you can so that folks will rally with you, and so that you can rally with them to get through to the policy makers who control so much of our lives. For example, look at the complete absence of anything humane that you can describe as city planning these days. You see what I mean? Whenever we try to talk about the most important issues, they go to something they call crime. I think the most important issues that most folks living in cities are dealing with have to do simply with getting through life, despite not having a plan that will facilitate that—let alone make that a beautiful possibility. I mean, our children are compelled to attend school—day after day—in buildings that are not only disgraceful to see, but also hazardous to occupy . . . and *useless* as far as what they impart. This is a bedrock difficulty that the youngest of us, the least able to fend for themselves, are having to contend with. And nobody's talking about that. That's the failure of what I call humane city planning to provide an inviting, safe, useful, and positive space for our children to become educated about themselves and the world. We don't have that! We not only don't have that on an institutional basis, we don't have that as a subject of conversation. And so I always ask myself as a poet and a teacher, "How am I trying to address these needs?"

DG Well, one of the things you have done as a poet and as a teacher is to create a class at UC-Berkeley, called Poetry for the People. Can you talk a little about this innovative class?

JJ It's an experimental program that's become very successful. It began at UC-Berkeley as separate classes of one sort or another—classes like African-American poetry or women's contemporary poetry or something like that. And then, in response to the students, I thought that what we needed to do was come up with a way for people to learn about poetry period. Then I wanted students to put their own poetry next to what's out there in some kind of way. And, at this point, it's been five years since the inception of that program.

DG Can you talk about the specifics of the course?

JJ As part of this course, we always have a component that is African-American poetry, but we also have two or three additional kinds of poetry that we try to come to understand—such as Asian-American poetry or Chicano poetry or something like that. And then we try to understand the worldview that underlies these traditions. So, for example, when we're about to study African-American poetry, everybody has to become familiar with Christianity. And, for example, this semester I'm teaching Arab and Arab-American poetry in which students are reading the Koran. I do this because I feel that otherwise you don't know why so many different poets from one particular tradition may always, again and again, seem to be taking a particular approach to—for example—suffering or to endurance or victory. What is that coming from? Well, usually it's coming from a collective worldview, and you often find out about that by studying the main religion of the folks you're trying to embrace as poets. And, then, I also require the students themselves to write an "African-American" poem, an "Arab-American" poem, and so on. In order to do this, they have to become familiar enough with the literature so that they're able to understand the characteristics—technically, and as far as attitudes and expectations go. Thus, they have to emulate those characteristics in a way that's useful to them in their own lives.

Now, that's all on the academic side. But there's another major dimension to Poetry for the People, and that comes fundamentally from the idea of "each one teach one." And so all of the students who join the program have the possibility of becoming teachers. That is, those who do very well in the very large class that I hold in the spring qualify to take a course with me in the fall called "The Art of Teaching and Writing Poetry." One of the requirements of that course is that you teach at either Berkeley High School, or at Glide Church, or on campus. You have to teach at one of those places, and most of the students actually end up teaching at two of these places. This is really an exciting part of the program, and—as you know—one of the best ways to learn something is to try to teach it. And through this whole process, students are becoming really incredible poets. Not only are they incredible poets, but they are incredible poets who intuitively understand that part of being a poet means community service—that being a poet is synonymous with community service.

DG How does this generation of poets compare with the generation of poets you came up with?

JJ The students I come in contact with are just so willing to take risks; they are so willing to work and create some kind of articulate political consciousness. It's very thrilling. For example, a young Arab-American student who is currently taking my class brought in a poem—

and the assignment was to write a poem about Ghaslah, which in Islam refers to the sin of forgetfulness, because in Islam there is no concept of original sin—the closest you can get is to forget that you come from God. So, anyway, she wrote this amazing poem that pierces your heart. The main idea is that Arabs and Arab-Americans are depicted so negatively that she becomes infuriated to the point where she finds herself separated from Allah—so this is a poem of grief about that separation. It's really powerful stuff. I mean, in this poem she has lines like: "You talk about terrorist and I only see the face of my father." And she concludes by saying: "I will become the monster that you see." So that one poem, which is less than a page, shows the power of this whole thing.

DG In collecting work for this anthology, I was overwhelmed with the amount of poems that poets sent me that had to do with "what's going on"; this chapter received significantly more submissions than any other chapter. What do you make of that?

JJ Well, a lot of people take their cue about what's going on from what they hear on television. And that brings us back to the role of the poet or artist. It's our job to say: "That's not what's going on—I'll tell you what's going on." And, for example, in the context of reforming our minds, this Islamic concept of Ghaslah could be revolutionary if we could get people to think about the sin of forgetting that God created you—hello! Knowing that, you know that you are fundamentally a good piece of work. But if you believe what people are saying about you, and if you accept how you are being depicted and described as pathological, you're forgetting that you're a great piece of work. And the Koran again and again makes this incredible argument on behalf of this idea. In other words, if you don't think that God created you, then how do you think you got here? You don't think that's miraculous? You know what I mean? I mean, if you wanted to come here again—let's say tomorrow—could you do that? *No!* You are a miracle, and you have to understand that.

And this is related to the loss of humane city planning; it's a loss of humane planning in general. You know, a plan about what kind of human being do you think you are . . . a plan about what kind of human being do you want to become . . . and a plan about what you need to get there. Let's put our energy there instead of putting all of our energy upon the so-called problems that are described to us. For example, if we allow ourselves to continue to focus on what's called crime, what's going to come out of that? I submit to you: absolutely nothing at all except an ever-increasing prison population—that's it. Crime is not a subject that interests me. I'm interested in finding out what would make young Black men from the ages of—let's say fifteen to twenty-four—really happy. What would make them really, really happy—happy and proud? Those are the questions that we don't have out on the table. Thus, I think as artists we're failing our people.

DG So what advice would you give to writers and artists to turn that around—to turn that *failing* into a *winning*?

JJ I would suggest that each one of you try to identify your purpose in being a poet—or painter, or dancer, or filmmaker, or whatever—what's your purpose? And if the only answers you can come up with refer to yourself, then those are the wrong answers. But if you answer that question and it carries you out into the world in a confident and dedicated way, then that must be the right answer. But if not, if it keeps you absorbed with yourself—not making connections and not helping anybody else—then that's not a right answer. I mean, when I was a young poet—younger than even you are, Derrick—I remember when I first went out to elementary schools to read poems. When I got there, students wanted to go to the bathroom immediately—because I was a *poet*. Now, I was hurt at first, but then I realized: "No, if I want these kids to stay in the room and listen to me and talk with me, I have to be listening to them—I have to be saying something that's interesting to them." And they are not going to be interested in me if I'm not interested in them—you know? So, if my purpose is completely self-centered or multiself-centered, that's not going to work; that's just not going to work.

AMIRI BARAKA

Of What Use Is Poetry?
(Babalu Meets the Wolfman)

What do you mean
    by Use?
Is there a
    second question?
And who are you, anyway,
    asking?
How did you get in here?
Are you laughing or crying?
Did you have a mother, a father?
Does anyone know you, beside yrself?
Can anyone see you, beside yourself?
Now, dont get beside yourself . . .
What was that question, again?
And put yr hands up!

KENNETH CARROLL

The Domino Theory
(Or Snoop Dogg Rules the World)

it is so clear
now
it was right in front of our
ears for all this time & only
now do we see

8

gangsta rap
gangsta rap did
gangsta rap did it

snoop dogg started the
transatlantic slave trade
doc dre was captain of a
slave ship & eazy motherfuckin
e lead the south to secede

it is all so clear
let the pundits come forth
let the congressional hearings begin
we have found the enemy &
they are dressed in chinos & plaid shirts
& county blues

gangsta rap did it
tupac was responsible for jim crow
it was ice cube not gov. Wallace that
tried to deny us equal rights
it was some forty oz drinking
jheri curl wearing
indo smoking
low riding conspirators that
pulled off watergate

will someone call NOW
gansta rappers,
screaming bitch, ho, skeeze,
defeated the equal rights amendments
will someone call c delores tucker
tell her we have found the enemy recording
on death row records backed by a funky ass

9

george clinton groove
it wasn't capitalism, racism, sexism, homophobia
hell naw

it was ice-t & ice cube & just ice
& all them refrigerated gangsta niggas
that screwed up america

spice 1 imported all the cocaine
to america, elect ollie north!
it was the south central cartel
that traded guns for drugs in nicaragua

before he died
eazy e bashed in nancy kerrigans knee
killed nicole simpson & ronald goldman
& caused the peso to plummet

let the pundits come forth
call jesse jackson
gangsta rappers are threatening affirmative action
call dick gregory
gangsta rap causes obesity & malnutrition
call ralph nader
gangsta rappers invented the corvair, the chevette, & the pinto

it wasn't hatred, greed or corporate america
it was niggas from compton, long beach, & the south bronx
it is so clear now
call louis farrakhan
gangsta rappers are the devil not white folk
call the pope gangsta
rappers are the anti-christ
leading us all along the funky road to hell
let the pundits come forth

gangsta rappers killed martin, malcolm, & both kennedys
they imprisoned mumia, geronimo, & peltier
they started the riots, caused the delay in the congressional budget
made hillary lie, spread the ebola virus, elected the republicans,
caused the challenger explosion & are responsible for your high electric bill

we were once blind,
but it is so clear now
ain't it good to know
now we can rest peacefully
as soon as we rid ourselves
of them o.g.s
ain't it good to know
let the pundits come forth,
the cameras are rolling.

KEITH ANTAR MASON

Friday Night

friday night
the bullet ripped
through torso
crack bone
entered lung
blood spurts
from lips
his teeth colored
he gurgles
he chokes
on 43rd
he is
seventeen

just turned
he just
learned
his length
he holds him
his manhood
the blood
seeps
he coughs
he wants
to spit
the bullet up
he hears
circle
envy
leaves
first
then
pride
the sky
gets
small
one
flash
light
beam
then
dark

She Should Have Called 911

The last episode
left her holding it
loaded
sawed off
and cocked
aiming straight
at the tip of
his manhood
He stood raw
looking right
in those cold
steely eyes
saying
"Wait baby,
wait girl,
you know its all good
now put the thing down
and quit trippin."
He stepped up
She stepped back
"Don't you fuck
with me Ray
I'm not playing
this time."
It was hard
to see outta
the bloated shut eye
she could move
her front teeth
back and forth
with her tongue

"Come on babe
It's me Ray
Your love makes
me go crazy"
and he took a step up
". . . but you're sweet
you need me!
you're my
tenderized meat
girl, you're all I got
good in my life."
and his lips
grazed her neck
until all her skin thawed
and her hands lost that
tense grip of hate
"Now see," he said slow
"this aint no way to be"
and she moaned
and he sighed
and it felt so nice
then he snatched
the thing
aimed close
and shot.

American Dialogue

*(for Michael James and Jackie Burden—residents of Fayetteville, NC,
   brutally murdered by two white American soldiers, December 7, 1995)*

this is my country too

[shoot those worthless niggers

worked hard enough to

give me the gun

claim ownership

shoot the bitch first

fought for their independence

poof.

as mine was denied

black bitch dropped like a bag of trash

believe(d) in truth and righteousness

damn, we should have fucked her first

justice will prevail

**shoot the black buck right between
those old big white coon eyes**

red is for the blood of our people

kabooooooooooooooom!

cursing the land.

**look at him begging and squirming in
his own pool of blood**

white still rules

DROWN, NIGGER

this is America

bwa-dop . . . bwa . . . bwa . . . urrh

you know.

NIGGER DIE!]

L.A. (Lost Assholes)

This town of lost assholes, L.A. it's called
as I look down from the guts of this heavy metal bird that U'M in
I feel uninspired by fascism and cops I know are down in
the futuristic wild west with the limitations and almost martial law
and Robots with Badges and Quick Draw Mc=Graw.

Just Lights and Glitter with Garbage underneath
And The Raging Oppressed With Razor Sharp Teeth.

KALUNDA-RAE

Hoochie Route

My homegirl
from
Uncle Tom's house
I took home
to my afro pickin' mama
She my mulatto prize
She the new ho
in my
pimpin' fortress
We be
workin' 2getha'
She on my team
Was
Was part of my kinship

Was
my sista' from anotha' (white) motha'

2getha'
we attended
freakniks
and freak weeks
fleet weeks
and freak meets
Went to Greek Fests
and club Essos
with high heels
and hooch clothes

Waited to exhale
with
one night stands
Spoke of
mack dreams
with
men in different lands

We fucked
niggas
wit' no scruples
crabs
and pimps wit' money in quadruples
ones wit' spots in limelights
(those that gave us chronic got to hit backs all night)
ones wit'
braids
bald heads

dreads
and perms
In dick we trust
In getting dicked
we learned
learned how to keep emotion
out of love
how to tell niggas
"thank you"
"get up and out"
learned how to jump in beds
without condoms
and feel no guilt
or hangover of doubt

But that's that
hoochie route
that I'm spittin' 'bout
That's our
hoochie route
and we do it
without a doubt

And if you find a future in my frontin'
I tell you how it used ta be
between her and me:

>Wearin' pink bobbi socks
>Our mouths aroused testosterone cocks

cause that's our
hoochie route
that I'm spittin' 'bout

That's our
hoochie route
and we do it
without a doubt

NIKKIA BILLINGSLEY

Rhetorically Speaking

Am I a ho
Because I love Black men
Because I love to love them
Whether I have one to 50
Is it a bad thing
If I've loved them wholly
In a certain space and time
Am I a ho
Because my hips move
With the rhythm
That rocks the worlds
Changes grown men
Into sleeping babies
Let me know
So that I'll point the next brotha
To a narrow-hipped, stiff walkin'
Asian or white woman
I have a hard time accepting the label
Because I choose my lovers carefully
Brothas needing love
A few with the rare ability
To love me
Sometimes I choose not to choose at all

Tell me
Am I a ho
Because I love myself and am free
To love others
I want to know
Why should I keep all this good pussy
To myself

ELAINE BROWN

If Randi Could Write

Part 1 (to be read aloud in a monotone)

New York Times, July 15, 1992, by Anna Quindlen:
"Randi Anderson's life story is sickening because . . .
commonplace . . .
Born to crack addicts,
reared in a tenement apartment with an empty refrigerator—
they would sometimes put a neck bone on the radiator
to heat it up for a meal . . .
She was difficult to love.
She stole,
drew on walls with lipstick
and defecated on the floor . . .
She had pigtails and big brown eyes and
once she ran in front of a car and screamed
'I want to die.'
She got a good smack for that.
She was five years old . . .
She was beaten to death . . .
by her foster mother's 20-year-old son . . .
[Her] mother, still on crack,

gave birth
last month
to another daughter . . ."

Part II (to be said aloud in your voice at five years old)

If I could write
I'd tell you it's been cold
five years on the streets
I never could remember
they names.
But I heard about 5th Avenue,
Madison.
And I seen, too,
on TV,
not just rich men
and pretty women
with furs
but food
You know.

And I was angry 'bout all that.
Okay, I was hurt,
and hurtin'.
But anyway, that's over
and I'm glad . . .
I didn't feel nothin' 'bout being a
poor
black
girl,
which is what I hear them callin' me
Voices.
Feeling sorry.
I understand,
really, I do.

I mean, I told you I wanted to die,
told everybody.
And it ain't nothin',
really,
dying.
I'm doin' it
easy,
better than anything.

Just like I didn't feel nothin' 'bout that doll
being white,
the one I saw
Downtown.
No, I'm lying.
I ain't never been Downtown.
But I saw
Downtown
in this book
in the Woolworth's or somewhere
I was stealing candy, or something,
and I saw that doll.
And I wanted to be her
not 'cause she was pretty
but 'cause she was wrapped up pretty
ready to go
somewhere
with somebody . . .

Anyway
I wanted him to hurt me.
I made him
'cause I was angry
at you
and hurtin'.

Okay, I was mad
at you, Mama,
'cause there wasn't anybody else
to be mad with . . .
I hope there ain't no heaven
I hope there's just sleep,
'cause I feel good now
he finally finished tearing up my ass.
But I wish I could ask you,
now,
before I can't,
why,
Mama?
Neck bones on the radiator and all that
and that's all . . .

Crack baby, they callin' me.
Mama's baby
I been trying to say
but they don't hear me . . .
I would cry but I won't
'cause you a bitch,
Mama.
Why you leave me for Baby Doo
I mean, Sonny
I mean, my daddy—though you never told me who that was
I mean, that crack?
I would try to tell you not to worry,
but I know you won't.
Nobody won't
worry
'cause I wasn't being born.
I was born.
Anyway, five years is over,

that's all I wanted to say
and
I'm glad it ain't gon' be five more.

　　　Part III (to be whispered in a low pitch)

I wasn't abandoned
I wasn't remembered
by ten million ossified brains,
just a feather disturbing
the fervor and swirling
of the clamorous stock
exchange.

It's a merciful man
who took hold of my hand
and whipped me so soundly
to death,
this silent surrounding
of nothing abounding
where I've finally come
to rest.

In the five years just passed
amid men and morass,
inside tenements grown
insane,
I overheard breaking
of souls in the making
and knew life was always
the same.

So I wanted to die,
with my mom by my side,
her sagging breasts filled with

cocaine,
and ask almighty God
why His terrible rod
always tempered my grief
with pain.
Ask Allah or Jesus
all of the reasons
why they never came when
I called,
why nobody nowhere
heard crying on stairways,
saw desperate drawings
I scrawled.

Statistically speaking
It's hardly worth noting
that I ever was born
or died.
And in this wide river
of infinite deliverance
I shall never again
ask why.

LETTA SIMONE-NEFERTARI NEELY

Rhonda, Age 15 Emergency Room

. . . Yeah, I been to juvee, what about it?
I was up at Spofford—they got legends
bout me—thought they wasn't gon git
rid a' me, but yo' I had to git de fuck up
outta dere, they had hoes that murder
people in that piece

and
I'm baaad and all but I ain't never
murdered nobody yet and I try not

to fuck up nobody too much less
they mama cain't recognize 'em
Last night, my man Ray-Ray, he 23
and built better than buster douglas
well anyway, we was over to his
crib and he was tryin to git on
for some
but he been locked up for 4 months
and I 'ont know what that nigga
been doin—shit, I know what
I was doin up in Spofford—
so when I tole him I was having my
menstruals, he decided to get plexed.
He smoked a blunt and wouldn't
take me home and den the nigga
went 'n fell asleep.
I was like damn, here I am
at Ray-Ray's crib and I got
a motherfuckin curfew and a
math test tomorrow (I'm tryin
to do good in school for probation
and dis lady who teach english
say I got potential—which I did
look up in the dictionary. It mean
I gots mad promise if my ass don't
end up in jail).

So I'm lookin for a pencil,
anything to write on which,
when I find it, is a paper towel
and thinkin that Ray-Ray ain't

helpin me none and he must
be a stupid nigga to boot cuz
he ain't got no paper and I
had to sharpen the pencil
wit a knife. I starts to think
bout findin me a new man
Me and my math problems
plexin each other to death,
when Big Mac come knockin.
He Ray-Ray's cousin
so I let him in. He say,
     where Ray-Ray?
I'm like he sleepin, he blunted out—
Ah, he say, *you wanna watch a movie*

I look at the napkin, crunch it
up, make a perfect 3 pointer and
follow Big Mac to the living room.
He put in the tape and turn off the
light. Then the movie come on
and at first I'm fixin to git up cuz
this ain't my kind of movie—girls
in all kinds of crazy positions suckin
white boys off, bitches lettin 'em
whip they ass and tie em up. That's
at first, cuz the next thing I know
I'm feelin crazy shit go through me:
     cunt juice drippin down
     my leg and I'm freakin
     myself out cuz i thought
     that shit only happen at
     Spofford. Cuz I'm imagi-
     nin I'm stompin all the
     white boys. Walkin up to
     em while dey whippin dem

girls and I'm stickin .45s in
dey backs—but that ain't all.
I'm thinkin after I kill 'em,
de ladies gon want to fuck
me, and yeah, that's the part
I'm trippin on, that I want them
to fuck me and that Ray-Ray
didn't never make me feel like
the cuties in juvee.

And I look over at Big Mac to see
if he know yet by the look on my face that
I'm a fuckin homo. Cuz if he don't know yet
I want to fix my face before he guess.
And when I look at him I'm like
I know this nigga done lost his mind cuz
the bitch is sittin there with his dick
outta his pants and his hand movin all
fast 'n shit and he stop when he see me,
den he start talkin real deep bullshit
he say,

> Rhonda come here, Why don't you
> do me, Come on Rhonda do me.
> Ray-Ray ain't gonna mind, I ain't
> gonna tell him.

He reach over and
touch me titty and me, ms. bad ass
all of a sudden cain't move
I'm frozen, I mean I couldn't move
> damn you cute
> girl, I wanna git my groove
> on wit you, I always . . .

The nigga
stop talkin then.

He all grunts and shit and I'm
imaginin I'm on another planet
tryin to think about the math test
and that lady-teacher I got
and I feel all that POTENTIAL
running the fuck away
cuz I won't claw this nigga to death
cuz I cain't even believe it's happenin
cuz he Ray-Ray's cousin and
cuz i ain't never felt no pain like this
so I don't feel it/I/think/bout/this/
time/I/beat/this/bitch/so/bad/she/lost/
6/teeth/and/got/scars/to/this/day/
from/the/box/cutter/I/slashed/cross/
/her/face/

I guess he done cuz he start to say
somethin

     don't worry girl, I know you . . .

And I don't hear the mothafucka
finish cuz I'm outta the room and
shakin Ray-Ray so hard he think
its a earthquake in Bed-Stuy.
I make
that nigga
git up
and take
me home
in his mama's
raggedy-ass hoopty.

And I start cryin
when I see my projects
and commence to tellin

Ray-Ray everything.
First thing he do is say,
  hell naw, you my bitch,
  ah'm a take care of this shit.

Den he tell me to take a bath
and he gon call me after he settle
this shit.
Then he leave.
I let myself in and hope mama ain't wake.
She ain't.
I go to de bathroom,
flick de light on,
watch de roaches git
de fuck out my way,
and set the water to run.
I wuz gonna take a real
hot bath, but I
membered too
late we ain't got
no hot water right now.
So, I pullt the drain
and went to bed.
But all I'm thinkin
bout is my test
and my potential—
how ahm gon git it back—
so I find the damn book
and jist study and study and study
till round bout 7:30 when
I'm still wide awake and
fixin to go to the school.

For the first time I'm gon
make first period.

I'm steppin out the door and I see
Ray-Ray walkin up,
he look real mad.
I don't feel nothin but
good cuz I know I can
pass. He git closer and I
smell malt on him. He say,
        I see you like them clothes, bitch
and I 'member right
then that I ain't changed
he say it again,
        yeah, you like the fuck smell on dem clothes.

I go "you crazy nigga,
I ain't like shit about yo cousin"
he like,
        you lyin cunt, Big tole me de
        whole story, He say you wanted to fuck him,
        He say you come over to him while he
        tryin to watch a movie and put
        your hand on his dick and
        He say he told you he wasn't gon'
        disrespect me like that but you kept
        touchin on him and I cain't blame the nigga
        for goin for his. I cain't believe you did that shit,
        Rhonda. You spose to be my girl and you go fuckin my cousin.

He got me backed up in
the corner in the lobby. People
see us and don't nobody say shit.
I don't say shit again cuz ahm in
shock and de only thing I'm thinkin
is bout how
to figure $x=y^2$
when he say,

You ain't got nothin to say, bitch?
the way to solve $x=y^2$ was
still runnin through my mind
when he hit me and I fell down
and I felt him kickin math answers
out my head.
I got sad cuz I wadn't gon' make
first period and my POTENTIAL
act like it ain't never comin back.

ASHA BANDELE

the subtle art of breathing

in the middle of everything i'm not doing   my doorbell rings it's the
landlady's lost son   i point him up the stairs mildly annoyed to have been
interrupted from my intent viewing of a soap opera   *one life to live* ironic
now that i think about it

nobody ever suspects women like me poets politically conscious   watch
soap operas but we do   at least i do grateful   to retreat into the
fictitious chaos of somebody else's life

but this is not a poem about soap operas

it's just that i cannot find another way to begin   i mean how   would
you do it?

would you start with a father's scream lancing the air
with the little sister's indelicate weep
or the acidic gurgle of a stomach in self-destructing
maybe you would simply begin like a broadcast journalist scanning a
teleprompter:

in anchorage today a 30-year-old black woman was found in her apart-
ment dead of an overdose. The incident has been ruled a suicide . . .

but this is not a poem about how to begin a poem
or a poem about lost sons and landladies
this is not a poem about soap operas

in islam they say from Allah we come to Allah we return leaving   the
curious among us hungry   for the story in between arrival and
departure   the person in the center   the thin arms desperate   to stop the
steady crush of closing walls   her first wall was daughter her second was
wife   not much room there to just be a woman   holy or unholy

but this is not a poem about religion

there are people who have accused me of creating the various & sundry crises
in my life   there are people who have accused me of refusing joy & of blan-
keting the sun   but then there are people who know as i know that even
as we laugh   we cannot ignore the wincing in our eyes   we are not
crazy or invested in sadness   sister was it that you knew there was no
space to be second best or needy in a country swallowing up the earth from
the inside out   they incinerate their own children here i have seen them
scraping   their own 8 year olds into garbage bags   or compactors
whatever's efficient &

it might be that this is a political poem

forgive me
i feel guilty   borrowing your family's pain   you were not my daughter
not my sister   i never even met you   your name & troubles were a
footnote   at the end of a discussion on lovers and where to go for dinner
that night   i know this space of mourning is not mine to occupy but i
cannot leave   your life reads like the details of my life   & i must
know why   you are dead   i am not   yet we both were 30
black female & fighting histories of drugs violence separation loss start stop

start stop again   we are a ritual of everyday blackwoman experience
stories repeated on sally & geraldo ricki lake & the news nothing unusual
suicide?

been there   done that &

maybe this is a poem about *déjà vu* or a poem about phyllis hyman or billie
holiday maybe this is a poem about my grandmother or your best friend from
back in the day   maybe this is a poem about you but it is definitely not a
poem about invented crises fictitious lives or retreating pretending lying
turning away or even praying

this is not a poem about soap operas

once i was told that i was more than all of my hurtings added up together
if i had known you   i would have told you that too   girl there
was more to you than your violent marriage   more than the brown girl
you became crouching   beneath dining room table   more to you
than the baby you lost or the last time you or any one of us gave ourselves up
like unwilling virgins to   cocaine vodka tonics cheap wine newports
colombian gold   & beer when the money got tight   girl there was clear
skin beneath your bruises   muscle behind the split ribs   a raving
beauty beyond *his* broke up sight & screams of *bitch lemme tell you something
you ain't shit nasty funky ass stupid ho*   & did you ever see her   even
once & if i did   & if i told you we were the same woman sisters maybe
twins   would you have been able to hear me

can i ask you something?

was this the first time you felt powerful? did you feel   finally some
control   did you say to yourself   can't be yanked out from under this
table   gotta hiding place that muthafucka won't never find me in   did
you think   at last   a truth no one will ignore   that the world will
believe you   now   i just remember feeling very calm

as i slid into pieces of the splintered wood of my dormroom floor all those years
ago   you know what would have happened if you had survived been
surprised by somebody coming back in after the 18th pill?   you would
have tried to fight them as they tried to make you walk   they would have
dragged you up & down the floors till the ambulance arrived someone
would have slapped you to keep you awake   whoever found you
might have read your journals   displayed your diaries   said they
just wanted to understand   at the hospital   if you arrived conscious
they would have made you eat a black chalk substance   to induce
vomiting   you would have vomited   uncontrollably   in front of
you   they would have stirred through it picking out the pills for analysis
    there is no other way to say this   besides i told you

this is not a poem about soap operas but

this may be a poem that warns   breathing is a difficult and subtle art   it
may be a poem to say simply   i understand sister   after 3 attempts
& 9 years past the last one   i understand girl   & i think this is a poem
that wants to assert itself   i'm proud even glad that i'm a survivor   &
sometimes when i am quiet & sometimes when i am alone & sometimes
when i am reflective & sometimes when i am scared & sometimes
sometimes when i am watching soap operas   i say oneday   i'm
gonna be even more than a survivor   i'll be a celebrant inside myself a
party girl in my own soul   i'll take myself out to fancy restaurants   bring
me roses   then make love to myself & in the heat of passion call out my
own name (asha, asha . . .)   yes   i'm gonna marry myself   does
that sound crazy?

martin luther king said *we may not get there together/but we as a people* . . .
& what if i do girl? get there   & find myself dancing wild in a bright silk
dress & high-heeled shoes   will you come too   ok   not now   but
your next time around   be your own sensual dance partner in
high-heeled shoes fine as hell girl   & so so so   fulla
life

Out of Pocket

messupmymind

the time?

da 9 soul is a lost and found
hound
dog
gin' me around

youknowwhatahmsayin'
?

i ain't playin'
just delayin'

the start of the minstrel show

yo bro!

you the head nig in charge

making war not peace
with yo-self

i wanna be where you are sam
right there on the stand with my man
oh-jay
cock-blocking the souls of black folks
sniffing glue with the spook who knocked down the door

you know

lifestyles of the rich and

shameless

survival of the fittest knee-grow

this side of the three mike
checks a one two a one two
y'all know what to do—

           it was thousands and thousands of years ago
             even way back before the first a-fro
ho!
ho!
yo' mamma is a . . .

tell me something good:
see delores run
see delores talk
see delores make simple rites into
a rap attack
not black
just wack
and stacked
with the loot of master
the smoothest blaster way before
krs-one kicked
criminal-minded
you been blinded
lookin' for a style like mine
and it's really yours

           i took it
           bit it
             fitted it
             kitted it
         now I own it
      zone it
    bone it
gonna bury it

but one tailspin from the hood ain't with it
ghosts of southern trees past
swing low
picking the lint out of toe
jams
at the 21st century mark

                                    hark! who goes there?

            it is eye superfly
                  the nig who will never die
comin' to make sweet potato pie out of
your left eye mister man

life ain't no big chess game
it's pitching quarters against the wall at P.S. 38

      my quarter clanging off the wall
and rolling back toward my holy sneakers
your quarter stuck in the crack that separates the
wall from you and the ants

      my pants riding the crack of my ass
            the way the world rides my ass
tight
right
quick
like a dick
punctuating
the right on right on
bombing of an american hunger
boom!

            self-destruction
we're headed for self-destruct—
a truck
fucks

with a boy with a toy
brain
trained
by the same mind
that said columbus went thisway
when he really went thataway
scoping out engines
talkin' 'bout

                  i discovered you all
             now get the fuck out of the way so i can
                   get on with my business
          and don't ask me about affirmative action either
                this ain't leave it to beaver
                    we meat cleavers

       chop chop chop
i be a cop
you be sagolee
spike lee
tupac if he was free
bigger thomas in a tree trying to pee
martin king squeezing free-
dom
from
cum drops raining on our heads
dead
we multiply and fry and lie and cry and try
this
and that's

             the way we do it

big poppa
can't stop a damn thing
not even the swing

of the clock
licking its snot
and blowing us down
to friday
thank god it's friday
chew on an ice cube and B-E-T
your life
your wife's
niece's
baby father
ain't gotta a quarter to toss against that wall
y'all
don't know what it's like to be a real trigger
with an imagination:

did you ever
stop
to wonder why
birds don't fly
very high
in the ghetto
?

it's a libretto for the bronze buckaroos
whose dues ain't enuf
to stop sam the man
hitting that grand slam

we die hard with a vengeance
especially while you were sleeping
french kissing casper
or was your name jasper
don't matter
you never feed him anyway
and he sprays on the wall
the way we used to tag graffiti

yes indeed-y
speedy
avoiding 5-0
pros with mo'
skills than a dollar bill
carrying half a gram of coke
it is the real thing
they bring
when the natives want out
and then the
boats can't shout
boss we sick & tired of bein' tricks on the high-wire—
can we go back home?

CHARLIE R. BRAXTON

The Gathering

on a quiet night
in death dealing dixie
jesus walks through the
smouldering ashes of what
once was the glorious house
of the lord
and sits on the charred
remains of a mourner's bench
moaning for those who have failed
the faith by refusing to fight back

Spirits Struggle

(For Eritrea, Somalia, South Africa, South Central . . .)

Sheba's sons slowly starve
as bullets like raindrops
harvest only blood's bitter aftertaste.
The strength is in the soul.
The sustenance is in the striving.
The survival is in the hope
that heaven will rain down mercy
on us now.

(. . . Rwanda, Burundi, Haiti, East Saint Louis . . .)

EL RIVERA

Elegy for a Martyred Poet

(For Ken Saro-Wiwa: poet, playwright, and brave leader of the movement for survival of the Ogoni people)

"TODAY, is a black day for the Black man . . ."
Today man played God and judged, judged artist guilty of
    resistance. Martyred for his beliefs, but charged with
      murder—Hang the judges for murder of thought!
Twisting a man's principle into levity!
Kicking principle, kicking beliefs—swinging submission,
    swinging transition;
      kicking yesterday, swinging no more tomorrows;
      swinging
      this mourning . . .

KAMAU DAÁOOD

Tears

I.

tears for the poet
swallowed by the cracks in the street
flowers for the dead musician
strangled by a bill collector in a bank parking lot
prayers for the painter drowned in white acrylic
what words for the dancer split apart in indecision

sacred heart, holy field of light
martyrs, healers

43

why does beauty wade through shit callused and unnoticed
why is the sweat of the heart invisible
why must love ache and peel in loneliness
like the orphans in trash bins of the world
dog shit on the jugular vein
the masterpiece submerged in the abyss of angels' blood
a painting hung on the wall backwards
lost to the eye of babies
why do sons die before their fathers
why do daughters give birth to children
with faces that add up to zero
as we sit in concert halls with chastity belts and earmuffs
promoters of robotic music cancerous and vile
mouth stuff with tombstones
mutilators of dreams

II.

batter rams spitting graffiti on uterus walls
watermelon seeds swelling in asphalt
traffic jams and drive-by shootings of pistol-whipped lovers
panting in the shadows, dancing in the spotlights of helicopters
woe to the lost fruit and all its nectar
woe to the suspended souls spinning in an unformed universe
crumb snatchers slip into a world of ice
wrapped in nightmare or AIDS tattoos and crack-smoked sunglasses
no eyes smooth, no navel smooth, no music, no mouth smooth
only nostril plugged with the funk of dreamless men
tripping over the length of their lives
scripted with a pitchfork at the edge of a flame

the place where they came together
is the place where they fell apart
they look at each other tongue-tied with pubic hair from coca-cola cans
in the void of cracked eggs chanting the pledge of alliance

to a pitbull with a billy club
on an ocean of crack vials and uzi shells
planned parenthood discussed in a think tank
when hitler became an American citizen
and hope floats in an empty pack of Kool
sailing down a gutter river of five million 40-oz. bottles of malt liquor
filter through the bladder of a ghost that is about to lose his pants

III.

holiness uttered from the bastard's lips
suck fire from ocean of stars in a drop of blood
to have been to the place of torment
and return with a badge of scars and praise on the lips

in the silence you will understand
when the ears are turned inward
and the work is placed on the desk of the heart
under the light of mind the soul sweats
eyes read the scripture on closed eyelids
you will extract wisdom from a tear
when the horses of desire are tamed and ridden to new horizons
then you will move through the body of god
as a healing agent
rather than a disease

Poem to the World

When lovers
on the brink
of
finding out
Recline on
fat illusions
of
their words
And utter platitudes
—instead of shouts
Forget
tender silences
they've shared
And all confession's
awkwardness they've dared
Like
children peeking softly from their doubts,
There comes a time
of
darkness and despair
When moments seem
like hours under weights
Regret and fear
like
garbage fills the air
And lips of fondest memories
turn to hate.

When lovers
on the brink
of

coming near
forget
the
body's swelled
and
aching cries
And
substitute excuses for their tears,
Something soft
and silent in them dies.
And
that, perhaps, is why there are old men
On benches
all alone
in city parks
And
bony-fingered spinsters with hard sad eyes
Knitting things for babies in the dark
And
maybe why we're lonely
in
the spring

When
all the earth her fat thighs opens wide
To show us all her pretty under-things
And
laughingly invites us to her side
To
kiss away the differences we've known
With the
tenderness
and
wisdom of her groans
Yet

We
lie beside each other
in despair
While
our bodies
make love
—in
the air.

DERRICK I. M. GILBERT (a.k.a. D-KNOWLEDGE)

Too Many

Back in the day
I don't remember goin' to
Or hearing about
Too many funerals
Except for when grandmas and grandpas
Died of old age
But
In this day
I see and hear about
Too many funerals
All the time
Funerals for victims of drive-bys
Funerals for victims of gang warfare
Funerals for victims of police brutality
And why are there so many funerals in this day
Funerals for victims of carjackings
Funerals for victims of drunk driving
Funerals for victims of reckless driving
And where are the funerals for folks
Dying of old age

'Cause all I see are
Funerals for victims of crack
Funerals for victims of nicotine
Funerals for victims of alcohol abuse
Funerals for victims of hyperstress
Funerals for victims of heart attacks
Funerals for victims of kidney collapse
And where are the funerals for folks
Dying of old age
'Cause all I see are
Funerals for victims of rape
Funerals for victims of spousal abuse
Funerals for victims of penis-driven patriarchy
And where are the funerals for folks
Dying of old age
Where are they
'Cause all I see are
Funerals for victims of aids
And
Funerals for victims of aids
And
Funerals for victims of aids
And
Does anybody have a cure for aids
'Cause I don't wanna go to any more
Funerals for victims of aids
And where are the funerals for folks
Dying of old age
'Cause all I see are
Funerals for victims of starvation
Funerals for victims of homelessness
Funerals for victims of hopelessness
Funerals for victims of suicide
And why are there so many funerals in this day
Funerals for victims of

White on Black
Black on Black
Black on Brown
Brown on Yellow
Yellow on Tan
White on Red
Red on Red
White on White
And
Everybody else on everybody else
Violence
Too many
Funerals for victims of
Everybody on Everybody violence
And where are the funerals for folks
Dying of old age
'Cause all I see are funerals for folks
Dying from going to
Too many funerals
Too many
Too many
Funerals
Too many
Too many
Dying
And
Does anybody
Die of old age anymore
Anybody
Die
Die
Dead
Dead
DEAD!

Poem for Derrick Gilbert

How many Indians?
How many Indians left?
How many Africans?
How many Africans now?
How many Indians?
How many Indians left?
How many Mexicans?
How many Mexicans here?
How many Jews?
How many Jews anywhere?
How many?
How many Catholics?
How many Queers?
How many Indians?
How many Indians left?
How many Muslims?
How many Muslim women and girls?
How many Indians?
How many Palestinians?
How many?

I can't handle the numbers

Who runs the lottery on what percent of who
ends up dead on the street
and
what are the odds that a drive-by
shooting will take out a 2-year-old
and her 15-year-old mother?
or
what is the cost of an LAPD surveillance

helicopter or an antipersonnel armored vehicle
for use in situations of civilian unrest?

And how many people
listening to these questions do
not have a clue
How many?
How many Indians?
How many Indians left?

How many minutes
How many hours before we agree that loving ourselves
does not require our hatred of somebody else?

I have someplace to go
and candles to light
and I live 3500 miles and 3
time zones away
from the only lover in the world
who can keep me
awake when I'm actually fast
asleep

And all of this hatred sorely aggravates my soul
all of this hatred aggravates my soul
and hate will not obliterate
3 time zones
plus 3500 miles
of Unadulterated Baby I'm Here By My Lonesome Self Reality
and so I'm trying to handle this math
I know
it's a fact
and there are these other
several happy things I want to find out about

instead
like
when will you love me enough
to move
just a little bit closer
or
my imagination of the snow that knows the furnace
of the secrets of your face
but
regular life feels difficult
feels fleeting and not
what
anybody (serious) could describe or
categorize
as SAFE
and so how about a political
meeting
a really big marathon
meeting
of everybody
tired of The President The Governor The Army The Marines
The cops
and white supremacy and racial purity
and religious and gender crusades?

How about a meeting
of (about) how many (would you say)
today?
How many Indians?
How many Indians left?

Chapter **2**

It's a Family Affair

AMIRI BARAKA

Derrick Gilbert What is the importance of writing about family?

Amiri Baraka It's not only the specific question—it's the general question. What you're really asking is: "What do I think about writing about ourselves?" And that's essential. I don't know how you can talk about anything else, you know, I mean at base—although there's all kinds of variations. But I think it's a basic kind of thing, and I think the question now is how do you take this superstructure back. You know, since the sixties, they've lied to us about everybody and everything. They have a book coming out every month lying about Malcolm or lying about Fred Douglass or lying about anyone else they care to lie about; today I even saw something about someone saying Sojourner Truth was crazy. So what they try to do is rewrite history so that the Black liberation movement seems like an illusion. They try to make it seem that Black people are not—quote—citizens because they're mentally and morally incapable of that. And so to try to counter the kind of endless outpouring of negativity about Black people/black families/black women/black men/black children, you have to begin with the actual base of who we are and what our lives have actually been. You must begin reflecting on the life of the family in the struggle.

You'll notice that on television you rarely even see a white working-class family, except maybe *Roseanne*—and I would be insulted with that image if I was a white worker. And with Blacks, maybe you see Cosby—arguing whether his daughter should go to Paris for a vacation. But the lives of our families, average families—people who have to struggle to send

INTERVIEW

you to school and who have to work vigorously every day—are never seen anywhere. Never! And that's the question that we as writers and intellectuals and artists need to confront. I hope that this new journal we're starting called *Razor* will help address these issues.

DG What exactly is *Razor*?

AB It's "Revolutionary Art for Cultural Revolution." We want a journal of polemic research and analysis. We want to throw out the canon—and the rock-and-roll museum and the Down Beat Awards and set our own standards. We want to define who we think is great and who we think represents our pantheon of excellence and achievement.

Tony Medina What was the poetic climate like in the sixties and seventies with the Black Arts movement, and how do you view this so-called new renaissance of new generation poets?

AB It's similar, because in the Black Arts movement we had all been raised in the backward fifties—you know, with the Southern agrarians and the dis-associations. Today you have the deconstructionists and it's the same thing . . . the whole idea about the world meaning nothing to literature. We had to deal with silly stuff like that—and you still see it. I even remember, some of the so-called beats, who I had a loose affiliation with, told me that Black writers can only write about Black people. We had to constantly deal with that kind of silly, ignorant, fascist, so-called anarchist doctrine. But we came out of that—we came out of that at about the same time as Cuba and Malcolm became prominent. We wanted to say finally: Look, we want an art that is identifiably African-American—that is based on our history and culture and experience. We want an art that is a mass art, and not some little elitist classroom kind of thing. And, then, we wanted an art that was revolutionary. We wanted rebellion art; we wanted art to reach people. That's why in 1965 we actually went out on the street every night with paintings on one corner and poetry on another corner . . . music on another corner . . . drama on another corner—we did that all summer.

TM Did that have to do with the popularity of what you were presenting?

AB Yeah, that's exactly what it was—'cause we brought the most advanced of the art. I mean we brought Trane and Archie Shepp and Sun Ra—you know, all those people. And people dug it . . . like we knew they would.

TM Now, what do you think is lacking today?

AB Institutions! Institutions! Institutions! Same thing that left us behind then. You see we don't create our own institutions and our own superstructure—we don't create our own journals and publishing houses. And if you can't actually carry out your ideas, then by default you will slowly roll back the hill into JoJo's arms.

DG But why don't we create our own superstructure when we seemingly have the resources to do so?

AB We might have the resources, but it's a matter of a people's point of view. Most people are so addicted to the image of being in America that they don't understand that they've never been in it. And, on the other side of that, they don't understand the strength in just being where they are. Look, if people exclude you from something, all it means is that nobody can go to them for you—they have to come where you is. So that's the strength of exclusion that we don't understand, and that's what Du Bois was teaching in the thirties and in the forties—that you have to turn segregation and discrimination itself on them. You have to set up your own networks, your own institutions, and utilize the commonwealth of the Afro-American people to build something that's self-determining and by that fact democratic . . . and by that fact, helps to build a true self-consciousness—because true self-consciousness in a practical sense is equality.

TM What problems did you experience when you had your own press?

AB Our problem was that we were so dead into the political activism in ways that we didn't have to be actually. A lot of the energy we wasted should have been focused on building those institutions and making them strong permanently. You understand what I'm saying? I mean it's important to be politically involved, but what we neglected is that we need to be more active in what we do. If we are writers, intellectuals, and artists, we need to be more active in doing that and getting that out. We need to find ways of getting our stuff out there: whether it's twenty-five-cent poems, or art showings in your garage, or theater in your basement. We need to tap into the spirit that animated black people in the thirties and forties—you know, with house parties and rent parties. We have to move forward cooperative, commonwealth sensibility. You know, we fight for democracy in America, but we have to be realistic about that. After all, if you want to fight for democracy in America, you need something to fight with.

DG Okay, with that construct in mind, what advice would you give to young writers today?

AB Well, first, write. Secondly, try to study something about all classes of people. Study the world as it actually is—cut through the bullshit. Understand the state of the art in all forms—whether it's dance, or music, or drama, or—for that matter—boxing. Understand what the most advanced form of anything and everything is. Then, you can use that collective information in your own work. Next, you got to publish yourself and start cooperatives and networks. You cannot just sit around and wait for the ghost to discover you and turn you into a spook.

TM One of the biggest obstacles is trying to make revolutionary ideas popular. And poetry is one of the ways in which you've done it and a lot of us are trying to do it . . .

AB Well, that's the point. That's the principal gig . . . is making advanced thought, revolutionary thought, accessible. But that's your gig—that's your job. You ain't got no other job that I know of. So if you ain't doing that one, the question is: "What is you doing?"

AMIRI BARAKA

Revolutionary Love

Black Revolutionary Woman
In love w/Revolution
Your man better be a revolution
for you to love him
Black Revolutionary woman
the care of the world
is yours, in your hands is
entrusted all the new beauty
created here on earth
Black Revolutionary woman
were you my companion I'd
call you Amina, Afrikan faith
and inspiration, were
you my comrade in struggle, I'd still
call you lady, great lady
Bibi, Black Revolutionary Woman
were you my woman, and even in the pit
of raging struggle, we need what we love,
we need what we desire to create, were you
my woman, I'd call you companion, comrade,
sister, black lady, Afrikan faith, I'd call you
house, Black Revolutionary woman
I'd call you wife.

Christmas Eve: My Mother Dressing

My mother was not impressed with her beauty;
once a year she put it on like a costume,
plaited her black hair, slick as corn silk, down past her hips,
in one rope-thick braid, turned it, carefully, hand over hand,
and fixed it at the nape of her neck, stiff and elegant as a crown,
with tortoise pins, like huge insects,
some belonging to her dead mother,
some to my living grandmother.
Sitting on the stool at the mirror,
she applied a peachy foundation that seemed to hold her down
to trap her,
as if we never would have noticed what flew among us unless
it was weighted and bound in its mask.
Vaseline shined her eyebrows,
mascara blackened her lashes until they swept down like feathers;
her eyes deepened until they shone from far away.

Now I remember her hands, her poor hands, which, even then
were old from scrubbing,
whiter on the inside than they should have been,
and hard, the first joints of her fingers, little fattened pads,
the nails filed to sharp points like old-fashioned ink pens,
painted a jolly color.
Her hands stood next to her face and wanted to be put away,
prayed
for the scrub bucket and brush to make them useful.
And, as I write, I forget the years I watched her
pull hairs like a witch from her chin, magnify
every blotch—as if acid were thrown from the inside.

But once a year my mother
rose in her white silk slip,

not the slave of the house, the woman,
took the ironed dress from the hanger—
allowing me to stand on the bed, so that
my face looked directly into her face,
and hold the garment away from her
as she pulled it down.

EVELYN E. SHOCKLEY

Oseola McCarty

eyes that see past self
a soul, like the swollen knuckles on worn, arthritic hands,
disproportionately large
a shy spirit that gave up schooling for family
and gave it back—one thousandfold—
to the daughters and sons you never had

a sick aunt to tend
then a washtub to add to you mother's and grandmother's
in the backyard
this bendingover onyourknees rubbingyourskinraw work
claimed your daylight hours
six days out of seven
it is hot in hattiesburg, mississippi
and you stayed tired
in every joint and every cell
but
there is always a day of rest
your grandmother taught you
there is always an hour of prayer

your mother assured you
such days and hours did come, year after year,
to keep your heart beating
and loving

over which tub of hot suds and dirty clothes—
perfumes of body odor and lye stinging your eyes and nose—
did you convince yourself that you
would never go back to school
never be a nurse, a typist
always do an invaluable job, undervalued?

full lips, full of prayer and bible verses
our godmother
you watched a little television
but rarely saw anything you wanted
except knowledge

three washtubs in a backyard,
then two, then
one
scrubbing hour upon hour
days filled with grass stains and soiled underwear
until, finally,
that living was lost to machines
and you began to iron

every Sunday,
you wore a nice dress and nice shoes to church
you heard a sermon
you sang a hymn

you praised the lord
o   my   soul
you put a little something in the collection basket
the same way, every Friday,
you put a little something in the bank
over the decades
there were bus and train trips not taken
modern conveniences not purchased
lovely luxuries looked at longingly and left in stores

today there is neither washtub nor iron
to steal your daylight hours
you sit
almost done with your life's work
resting your roughened hands quietly in your lap
you pray
you thank God for your life
you pray
think of your savings,
the pennies and dimes and dollars deposited over the decades
you will live on it while you live
you arrange for the larger part of what remains
to go to the local university
for your godchildren to use
i'm saying
a $150,000 scholarship fund for black students
the rest to your church
i cry

hands that give, though stiff
eyes that see past self

Lovesong to My Father

I remember bathing with you
in the deeps of Big River
after your long absences overseas—
your presence strong, deft
as we splattered and plashed froth
snapping our frazzled towels
in cracks of delight. And, oh,
that cricket game, your pace

ball cornering my privates—
the bite of a thousand fire ants,
but I scored—you said I scored.
And at the airport on that summer,

you held me—held me firm,
when I feared the snake-rippling
escalator. I loved New York that sky-night:
a colossal chandelier, too bright,

too fresh and electric for your
proper, Back-a-Yard son who,
once we finally touched down,
would stay in—study home—till Daddy

returned on other people's schedules,
only then would I go out, only then
to the library. I remember kissing
your big lips chalky with Winston Regulars,

and rubbing against that two-day shadow
with room enough for friends—gruff
and frank, like the brush on Papa's
weekend pigs. I barely ate pork then

but always scalded, always shaved the kill.
And now returns that foreign time,
my flapping heart, your lovesome will.

PAULA WHITE-JACKSON

Saturday Morning Pancakes

In his kitchen
STANDING TALL
flipping pancakes high
in the air
for his captive audience
4 little girls giggling
mesmerized
as Daddy performed
stacking up
golden-brown pride
maple-coated dreams
wishing every day
was Saturday.

Artichoke Pickle Passion: Sonnet

In southern springs we dug for artichokes
In Miz Olivia's tall and weedy yard.
She dipped her snuff, but never, ever smoked;
At eighty-five, she wasn't avant-garde.
Her 'bacco spittings grew the vegetable;
Well nourished were the tubers, strong, the stalks.
And even though their worth was questionable,
With hoe in hand, we dug, postponing talk.
Once washed, soaked, sliced, they met some torrid brine.
Aromas flew on steamy clouds of heat.
When canned, the waiting was the longest time.
How many weeks or months before we eat?
In southern springs, we dug the precious root,
And still, this day, it is my passion fruit.

Familee Reunion Tyme

familee reunion tyme iz a special tyme
where all tha kinfolkz from far & near
simpli gather 2 celebrate
anotha year of familee life
where all tha kinfolkz from far & near
gather 2 add new branchez of hope & spiritual
foundation
2 that familee tree & stuff
now can u feel my flow
cuz uc

familee reunion tyme is a special tyme
2 reminisce & swap ole storiz
bout/once upon tyme & bak in tha dai &
who did what & whoop te whoop
bout unclez & auntiz
& grandma & grandpa
& momma & daddi
& brothaz & sistahz
& 1st cuzinz & 3rd cuzinz
who claim 2b cuzinz
who ain't realli/realli cuzinz
yet they mite b distant/distant cuzinz
twice remov'd ova from tha 3rd side
now can u feel my flow
who've all gather'd that 1st saturdai
in August/of course
2 eat large helpinz
of sweet potato pie/blak-eyed peaz
lima beanz/mustard greenz/countri fri'd chicken
& deep fri'd catfish/with louisiana hot sauce
homemade corn bread/from scratch/of course
with plenti of rice & gravi
pass tha yamz pleazeee
& all tha bbq & peach cobbler
& banana puddin pie yo stomach can desire
now can u feel my flow
cuz uc
familee reunion tyme iz a special tyme
where all tha kinfolkz from far & near
simpli gather that next dai/on sundai
2 worship in GOD's house/az one
az mani tearz are shed that final dai
az we must say our last goodbyez
2 allll tha kinfolkz
knowin in our heartz that we mai neva

eva again c tha luv onez
that GOD mai chooze 2 make
that final journei/home 2 tha promis'd land
now can tha congregation sai/AMEN
yet & still we find comfort & peace
knowin in our heartz that a special tyme
waz had by all
i mean/knowin in our heartz of heartz that a veri
special tyme
waz had by all tha kinfolkz
who came from far & near
that 1st saturdai in August/of course
2 attend that traditional
southern familee reunion
now 4 tha veri last tyme
can tha congregation/pleaze sai/AMEN

NIAMA LESLIE WILLIAMS

Companion Pieces

One

dishes dried,
i curse that he is not here.
i am only twelve
and carry much on my shoulders.

i have cooked the evening meal
and they laughed at my too small, too hard burger.
mother shushed them
but brothers will be brothers
and persevere.

it is my turn to dry the dishes
and i do so alone.
they are permitted to work in pairs.
they gang up on me often
i lie in wait
my turn will come.

mother asks for the meat platter
on which to defrost tomorrow's debacle.
i am nearly through,
the dishes stacked neatly, carefully,
measuring cups inside teacups inside bowls inside pots
glasses on the outside—
but she wishes the meat platter.
it is buried.

i reach for it and the dishes tremble.
a pot shifts place.
i pull it out, and the change in balance causes the dishpan to rise,
waver,
then tip over.
all the dishes clatter to the floor
i watch them break in midair.

nothing has felt this good.

Two

he doesn't hear the dishes shatter
but wonders what his twelve-year-old was thinking
as she watched them fall.

"she just stood there
then walked out of the kitchen!"
his ex-wife's voice borders hysteria

she is asking for money to replace the dishes
it was Thanksgiving
we are talking china here.
he wonders at burgers on Thanksgiving
at not being there to taste his daughter's first meal
he knows he has deserted her in an unfriendly household
he no longer understands what to say to his sons
to make them kinder
he has recently married
and they have made themselves off-limits.

he remembers his twelve-year-old's face
and worries
the anger is buried so deep
she is trying so hard

he thinks he has heard
the first explosion.

MERILENE M. MURPHY

Fat Grass & Slow Rain

(For Willene & Walter Murphy)

moonlight's a slow rain
hands cupped twice & lips

daddy kisses my toes

our secret runs red twists red
our secret runs ma's fat grass
our secret runs   jumps loud spring

he listens for flowers at ma's navel
my ears   flowers
my fingers   flowers
my mind

i track his voice down
march 20th
first day of spring 1955

ma's a red moon we turn
ma's a red skyburst six a.m.

he kisses my toes
through ma's red belly
i catch his face by voice

moonlight's slow rain
& stars
i am kisses

amber bliss
i explode between them
fat grass & slow rain
i explode between them
flowers
    . . .

he never said much
after i was born
except
hey pumpkin
here's math

a hundred years after
i was born
when i was 19
he evaporated

moonlight's slow rain
he went

he never said much
after i was born
except
what you need

here's love
here's loaf
he walked with a stutter

he walked with a stutter
to d.c.
all the way to jail
for me to speak free

here is loaf
here is love

he walked with a stutter
but i feel him now
loud & clear
carrying me
  . . .

now fat grass loves her some slow rain
let me tell you
fat grass lovers her slow rain even more

i ain't never lied
grass & his green eyes want to be water
slow rain & she wants to dance
hands cupped twice & lips
i am just a thought

a dance between them
their suburban eyes on a bus

i guess you could say
except for the dancing
i am where they stop
to think about
the next
step
 . . .

it's count basie's dance floor
basie's the best
pumpkin
it's the count
slow rain is six feet & green eye vicious
& me
i'm just a thought
bouncing around on count's dance floor
waiting for moonlight's slow rain & fat grass
to take root
hands twice cupped & lips
waiting for moonlight's slow rain & fat grass
to take root
in my song

Tanka

grandmama frying
black skillet full of catfish
this wet afternoon
big brown boy sucking fishbones
and leaning over the sink

Haiku

a black woman
breast-feeding her infant—
the autumn moon

Haiku

morning fog
my daughter dropped off at camp
fumes of city bus

MAIISHA L. MOORE

Haiku

the dark rock-road
a car coming down it,
    me and my daddy

BRIAN GILMORE

Hazing

(For Tony New and Albee)

i once pledged
my father's fraternity.
the day he came
home from work
unexpectedly
and caught me and my friends getting
high in the basement

through the thick
smoky haze of the best
panama red i had ever tasted,
my father happened to see his
red and white kappa alpha psi
paddle sitting in the corner.
gripping his paddle tightly,
dad immediately placed me on line

despite the fact that i never
expressed any desire to join his
or any other fraternity.

the pledge period lasted
all of ten hits
as i ran through the
thick
cosmic clouds of smoke
that i had been enjoying only
a second ago,
out the back door

off line

away from one of those
brothers who takes this greek life
thing a little too serious,

never to get high in the house again,

never to cross those burning sands . . .

MAWIYAH KAI EL-JAMAH BOMANI

Homecoming

there was a knock
at the door
and she answered

he said

"honey i'm home"

she said

"listen baby
touch
if
u will
but
this here body
it ain't got
no open-door policy
the day u walked out
i changed
all the locks"

E. ETHELBERT MILLER

Mountain Wife

in the yard
the truck sits stuck in mud
the hood bleeding from the last accident
I tell Carrie not to play near her daddy
not when he drunk or can't find work
I yell at her but she can't hear
ears deaf from my own screams
I wash our clothes with my tears
the hardness of my hand like his
I pass the mirror in the bedroom

and I recognize my mother's face
my husband sleeping in his clothes
just like my daddy did and now I dry
between my legs while praying
his spit won't make me pregnant

M. ELIZA HAMILTON

Things I Do Not Speak

My mother is 49. She has been dying for four years.
No one knows why.
She cleans my room, puts new doilies on my dresser.
She makes sure I have clean panties.
She finds my diary, reads it, discovers my life,
makes me destroy it in front of her. To be sure.
She does not understand my silence.
I do not explain.
I do not say thank you when she puts out the fire in my hair.
She says, You never miss the water till the well run dry.
I am 14.
I am not supposed to like my mother.
And I don't.

My mother is 98 pounds. She does not leave her bed.
Every six weeks they give her someone else's blood.
She does not bake Christmas black cake
after soaking the fruit in rum.
She does not laugh, tell my sister stories,
or wear her favorite purple pants.
The police bring her home. She is so tired.
Strangers bring her home. She cannot walk by herself

from the bus stop, the corner.
A boy my age helps her home with groceries
to the bottom of the stairs.
I hate him. I hate walking with her in the rain,
anywhere at all. She walks so slowly, is so weak.
She does not want to lean on my arm, but must.

Thanksgiving days I hate cooking turkeys.
I hate lemon-yellow Samsonite overnight cases
already packed, telephone calls to doctors,
good-bye kisses that taste like death. I hate needles,
hospitals, green hallways, illness and its stagnant flesh
rotting smell. I hate the sound of my father's keys at seven P.M.
I hate the feel of darkness and alone entering my soul at 7:01.
And never leaving. I am afraid I will get sick too.
I hate pain most of all. I count down to her age.

My mother is dead. I do not know why.
I do not cry at her funeral.
I get pregnant in her birth month.
The woman who holds my hand during the abortion is not my mother.
I am looking for a woman to be my mother.
I am looking for a woman.
I want only a woman.
I am looking for mySelf
I keep coming back to her.

Biological Didn't Bother

Yo Yo
I want to dedicate this song to
Phillip Arthur Harrison
Word Up!
'Cause he was the one who took me from a boy
To a man . . .
So as far as I'm concerned
He's my father
'Cause my biological didn't bother.

Biological father
Left me in the cold when a few months old
I thought a child was greater than gold
But I guess not
You brought me into this world but you're not my dad
Mess around with them drugs
Made my moms mad
So we left you
No remorse or pity
Took the first bus from Newark to Jersey City
Raising a child alone . . . now that's pressure
Moms gotta go to work
Drop me off by Odessa
Mona
Aunt Beevie
Whoever
Aunt Thelma
Uncle Roy
We stuck together

A year went by . . . and I can walk y'all
Moms got that good ole job at City Hall
She probably didn't trust men anymore
Until Phillip Harrison walked through the door
Went out a few times but what about Shaquille
Mom offered him a million-dollar package deal
She said you want me
You gotta take my son
Or else it's like a hot dog
But without the bun
Guess what?
He accepted
Responsibility . . . he never left it
He kept it
He kept it
He took me from a boy to a man
So Phil is my father
'Cause my biological didn't bother

He took me from a boy to a man
So I always had a father
When my biological didn't bother

Phil is my father
Phil is my father

January 5
Phil made a promise
He joined the army
We moved to Ft. Monmouth
He disciplined me right from the get-go
Age two bottle in my mouth
Shaquille let go

Actin' spoiled
Rotten
Trippin'
Gotta butt whippin'
Because I didn't listen
Back then you see privates made no bucks
Had to get another job
Driving trucks
Working hard as hell didn't satisfy him
Had to get another job
Working at the gym
He wasn't gone with the wind
Like Clark Gable
Worked all them jobs to put food on the table
Phil's my father
Daddy!!!
And that's the scoop
Can I go to the gym with you
And shoot some hoop
Come on . . .
He put me under his wing
Was the ball boy for his local army team
Sometimes he even made me mad
But that didn't matter
'Cause I still wanta be like Dad
But to a little bit better
Encouraged me to stay in school
And to get them good letters
I wasn't a brainiac
But I tried hard
Got to watch the Knicks play
If I had a good report card
All types . . . all sorts
Disobey my dad and I couldn't play sports

I learned to dribble from right to left
I couldn't do a damn thing
With all them F's
Age 15
Father-and-son confrontation
That's nothing
But father/son trials and tribulations
Back then I couldn't understand
But I'm glad he did it
'Cause now I'm a man
He took me from a boy to a man
So Phil is my father
'Cause my biological didn't bother

He took me from a boy to a man
So I always had a father
When my biological didn't bother

Phil is my father

Look at me now
Successful for sure
Phil raised me well
To be an entrepreneur
And if you make it big don't be materialistic
'Cause you'll end up just another statistic
Everything's going well . . .
Following my dream
I dunked on Patrick Ewing
I want a ring like Hakeem
Oh Oh . . . what do ya know
Biological one's on the Ricki Lake show
What does he want???

Does he want money???
What—people—do—for—MONEY!!!
It's kinda funny to me
Huh . . .
He ain't gettin' no check from me
Check it
He can go on all the talk shows he wants
Phil is my dad . . .
So don't even front
He took me from a boy to a man
So Phil is my father
'Cause my biological didn't bother

NADIR LASANA BOMANI

Thin Water

it was a foreign night
your breath wore liquor
your slurs sluggish
you spoke a language i
did not fully understand
ranting
screaming some shit about
   "you do as i say."
"you're not my father!"
i yelled back
not to say the one who is acts like one
but i do not claim strange men just because
my mother discovered them
even if they live here

my words raped your manhood
your eyes blew fire
tension danced in our silence
rudely the sound of
thunder cut in when the force
of your fist caved in my chest
the destructive roar lured my
mother into my bedroom
i plunged frustrated
to a floor that knew
i would not get up
to fight you
i wanted to kill you
when he sleeps
a knife will kiss his throat
i thought
my mother made you leave . . .
she saved your life

V. KALI NURIGAN

I'm Raising Children

i'm raising CHILDREN
i'm not the farmer's daughter
raising CHICKENS
to be slaughtered
not the sharecropper's child
raising CANE to be
CUT DOWN
i'm raising CHILDREN here

RAISING

not california singing dried fruit
raisinettes
not raising STRANGE FRUIT
to hang from some oppressor's tree
i'm raising PRECIOUS fruits
to grow HIGH on the vine
PRECIOUS FRUITS reaching toward
the sunshine
raising the fruits   of my womb
to multiply   by fives
to stay alive
i'm raising CHILDREN here
no little bo-peep
leading her sheep to be slaughtered
these are my daughters
these are my sons
i'm raising CHILDREN y'all
raising them UP
ABOVE the floodwaters
I AM the crossing guard
cross me and YOU'LL be sorry
'cause i'm raising CHILDREN here
between rock and hard space
betwixt slim and none
'tween fatback 'n' no slack
i'm raising CHILDREN y'all
the instructions are included
DON'T FOLD SPINDLE OR MUTILATE
the instructions BEEN included
DO NOT FOLD SPINDLE OR MUTILATE
NEGLECT MISUSE OR ABUSE
just follow the instructions

like you do OGUN OSUN and the

MOON

just follow the instructions

cause i'm raising CHILDREN here

i'm raising CHILDREN y'all

i'm raising CHILDREN here

HAKI R. MADHUBUTI

A Bonding

(For Susan and Khephra, August 20, 1989)

we were forest people.
landrooted. vegetable strong.
feet fastened to soil with earth-strengthened toes.
determined fruit,
anchored
where music soared,
where dancers circled,
where writers sang,
where griots gave memory,
where smiles were not bought.

you have come to eachother in wilderness,
in this time of cracked concrete, diminished vision, wounded rain.
at the center of flowers your craft is on fire.
only ask for what you can give.

do not forget bright mornings, hands touching undermoonlight,
  filtered
water for your plants, healing laughter, renewing futures. caring.

your search has been rewarded, marriage is not logical, it's necessary.
we have a way of running yellow lights, it is now that we must claim
the
sun in our hearts. your joining is a mending, a quilt.

as determined fruit
you have come late to this music,
only ask for what you can give.
you have asked for eachother.

chapter 3

No Ordinary Love

NTOZAKE SHANGE

Derrick Gilbert How would you define love poetry?

Ntozake Shange I think of all poetry as love poetry. I mean, to observe, and to accept and to take the time to note the specificity of a thing, with delicacy, whether it's passionate or thrashing, is a kind of love. I think art is a way of making love in general. So that's one answer . . . well that's the only answer I have actually. All poetry is love poetry.

DG What was the poetic scene like when you first got involved performing and publishing poetry?

NS I think that right before I came onto what you call the "poetic scene," many poets—and even Black women poets—were caught up in the revolutionary zeal of the moment. That is, their poems often were not looked upon as poems about real people. Instead, they were poems about the warriors . . . and the queens . . . and the kingdoms . . . and the heroic survivors of our holocaust. Now, a lot of that work was very beautiful and profound, but it often didn't look at the specificity of people. But with luck and good timing, and a lot of hard work, I was able to produce work that forced us to accept ourselves as more than a mass of people—more than just a mass of energy. With my writing, I wanted us to see that we are an amazing collection of individuals with multiple and miraculous intricate stories to tell—stories that are generations old and intergenerationally dependent . . . that have to do with love lost and love gained.

DG How did people initially respond to your approach to poetry?

NS Well, I think that because the Western cultures are so male-dominated—and that African Americans often seemed to follow suit in terms of the arts—love or romance poems were viewed as having diminished significance. So at times some fool might come up to me and say something foolish like: "Why you writing love poems?" or "Why aren't you writing more about the struggle?" And that was kind of idiotic. We have to fundamentally understand that, for a people, the perpetuation of love and family is essential. Oftentimes, your oppressors understand this better than you do. Take, for example, all the laws during slavery that were passed so that we couldn't marry who we wanted—or sometimes we couldn't marry at all. They also have done this in other countries all around the world. You see there is power in love and coupling, and often those who are most victimized by some sort of oppression don't fully realize this power.

DG I would like to change the subject for a moment and ask you if you think that rap is poetry?

NS Yes, of course! I've always felt that rap was a genre of poetry; but I'm also starting to lose faith in the positive potential in rap. You see, I used to have high hopes for the rap genre—I even put aside my resignations about some of the things I was hearing in rap. Specifically, I wasn't as critical about the sexism and misogyny that was prevalent in a lot—not all—of rap. I did this because I understood their rage. Actually, I felt—and still feel—that I have the same connection to rage as they do. I also feel that the rappers are very passionate—and that revolutions are ultimately built on passion. Unfortunately, I haven't seen a significant amount of growth within this genre. But I haven't completely given up on it . . . and I think there are some positive, nonsexist, revolutionary poets out there.

DG What advice would you give to young writers and poets today? And I include rappers within that question.

NS My advice is to immerse oneself in the histories, as we know them, from all over the world—in order to understand the place we live. That means we need to study such things as the Aztec and Mayan empires, the rise of the samurai, the evolution of monasteries, the contradictions of Peter the Great—anything, everywhere at all times . . . and as much of it as you can get your hands on. But don't just read the history—also read the fiction and poetry . . . and look at the artifacts and architecture of whatever interests you.

DG Can you elaborate on that last point?

NS In other words, one cannot come to a poem or a painting as a creator empty-handed. We have a gift and/or burden of more than ten thousand years of human history—of which we are the current manifestation. Therefore, if we have any respect for our elders, if we have any respect for ourselves, it's important to know what we're talking about. It's essential that we are able to glean from multiple sources—the various images, or analogies, or symbol systems that are appropriate for the piece we're working on.

And I have to end by saying that I find it extremely condescending and dangerous to assume that those of us who haven't had access to what we call "higher education" must be addressed simplistically. Or that they must be confined to what we think that they only know. The collective unconscious defies that kind of thinking, and the human imagination belies it. So I would say to writers, young and old, to tap into your unpoliticized feelings and always let your imagination . . . and the imaginations of others, fly.

NTOZAKE SHANGE

The Lizard Series

a dogon iguana
one eye openseeing me
seeing my dreams
creep like david
rousseve's feet
from my finely cut
pecs   rahway built
niggahs on gleamin'
bridges admireso
much they stop
smile snaggletoothed
gleamin' lust gleamin'
all they know i bettah
not toy wit/dreams

swimmin' top the
rio grande in
rainy season/so
my calves tease
the border patrol
"jalisco courtin' dance?"
"no, sonora harvest"/toes
water ritmo/made it
land tattoed like
his arms lizards
slitherin' on top
the wet crossin'
toward acaba

toward me like
silk his skin demands

a human touch
can you smell it?
the pimiento & dust
lettuce & uva now
hard as muscle his
lips dawn permanently
gainst steam
rushin' from
dark patterned family
espresso pots
"papi, esta listo" como
some four-legged
underwater creature
lithe 6 million years
old a conspicuous
choio agasao

when he quotes
marti nobody notices
but me by the
Malecón hidden in
tides risin' with
each morena's wall
etched on our skin
how cd she know
guillen the tricky
cubano light on
his feet/a black
ox covered with
ribbons & bloody medals
for his amazin' grace

how el son trips
sacred from his
laughter & la havana

vieja rolls her
eyes cause once
these words fragile
full of coney island
bubbles float from
mouth to nose
to miami the torture
negrita in santo dominga
whose mami sewed
polyester hems while
trujillo imitated
porfirio's dreams of his
own statue/
loose rice powder round
the dark brow the
lizard stretches
one limb toward
mahogany branches
born away by many
poets tired and lonely

one water buffalo
yearning for one
chord from yomo toro
the lizard on the
other side of the
border whose breath
blends with hibiscus
sweet tequila &
my hair/lizard closes
his eyes/skin now
roughened crepe/
limbs cut-buddy
to gallopin apaches
outside denver/nestled

painted by trunks
of carved trees/R.I.P.?/
that leave the Grand
Concourse a great
fiesta or new orleans
funeral trails/we
smell each other from
separate territories

my scent confines me
to specific sails
far from the
swamps & rivers
the lizard traps my
ankles without a
sound the pouch
taut round some
one's mouth fallen
open/"the cafecito
is sweet/sí papi"
when I wiggle slowly
seeking my natural
state of repose
my skin is silk
    to touch
tattoed/a dogon
iguana in her
own soft-boned
splay/ but not
actually/I'm
over/there/no over here/I
crossed the border
right under yr
    eyes

101

Love

And he took your hands
and gently placed your body on the canopy bed
There were roses and Cassiopeias spread over the sheets.
The smell of myrrh and sandlewood made your bodies hotter
He rolled you over like hot bread
and peeled a mango on your back.
He started eating juice dripping not knowing whether it was sweat
or the ripe juice.
"Baby I want to see your face"
He turned you over slowly the mango juice racing down the nape of
your back
You were ready to take his manhood
but you wanted him to gently open you up to work a little
you was going to savor this feeling
You let him in and the rhythm came,
It came strong and from some other place
The curtain at the top of the canopy gently moved with air

But instead of canopies you find yourself being pushed up against a
brownstone window, people walking by.
"It ain't none of my business"
Instead you find a knee in your pregnant stomach
Instead of sandlewood and canopies there is spit in your face.
Generations of dysfunction that has to be released like stale
spittle

Yvell, where are you?
Are you here being abused your dreds being pulled out
This hair that now gives you power
Which used to choke like rope from around the necks of our

mothers and fathers and sisters as we hung from trees
This mango is a strange fruit

Yvell, where are you
are you in Togo getting a forced clitorectomy
or maybe you're a child in the Delta being touched by a dirty old
man

Yvell, where are you
under the table trying not to get hit

Yvell, where are you
as we sit in your car on the way to work we cry
I want to know why I have cancer you want to know what kind of
situation you've found yourself in.
A history of dysfunction
A history of dysfunction
A history

Take these antiquated rhythms and make new ones
Listen to the drums
Push new blood through your veins
Be fierce girlfriend
and love your child
love your child
love your child

K. CURTIS LYLE

Your Tears Feel Good on the Hood of My Car

Your tears feel good
On the hood of my car
Preserving the shine
That I worked so hard

So hard and so long
Creating my car
The miraculous me
At this frequency
Preserving
Safekeeping
Maintaining
And seasoning
My car

That's why
Your tears feel good
on the hood of my car
Your hands feel good, too
Because they know what to do
How to keep me intact
With one protean act
I'm in love as I fall
Into total recall
The full moon in me
At this frequency
Preserving
Safekeeping
Maintaining
And seasoning
My car

Your body feels good
On the hood of my car
Confessing to me
That you want to feel
What's under the hood
What feels better than good
Where dreams can come true
If you know what to do

A whole new frequency
Inside of me
LOVE ME BABY
Preserve me
Maintain me
Protect me
Don't taint me
Reason and season
The engine
Up under the hood
OF MY CAR

Up under the hood
Of my car
We can stop time
Up under the hood
My engine is primed
Up under the hood
It ain't no crime
To disappear for a while
To make love to me
With power and style
The world record's not far
See things as they are
Make love to me, baby
Up under the hood
Of my car
DON'T FORGET BABY
Preserve me
Protect me
Maintain me
Don't stain me
Reason and season
The engine
Up under the hood of my car

Sat. Nite

There's this womun I call
on Sat. nite cause she my Sat. nite drinking partner
we stay up all Sat. nite long
& laff & touch drinking & talking about
important stuff like pastry & finger painting & how crazy folks be now days
& I really like her cause she kool &
got a body that a bad poet
might call overripe and she got
this cat with shiny black fur
that she let me rub on sometimes so Sat. nite we rub on cats fur
& talk & drink gin & pass out watching old movies & each other making sure
   we
stay safe cause
being drunk on Sat. nites kinda dangerous
sometimes so we take care of each other
on Sat. nites & we aint even sexed yet
but we gonna cause I like her & I think
she like me too cause
one Sunday morning buttnaked & hung over
she held my head up over the toilet bowl
when I couldn't do it for myself & you gotta like someone to do that for them
   so
we gonna do it eventually
but one of us always seems
to pass out before we get
around to it but it's all right cause
I like her & I don't want to be drunk when we do it cause I want to know
   what
when I'm doing it so I can tell my

pops everything & when I drink I like to get drunk & sloppy
& I want to be smoove
when I'm doing it with her
cause she my Sat. nite drinking partner & she deserves it done right.

WENDY L. JAMES

Troy

I celebrate the power in your eyes,
their flexing aptitude for crushing pain.
The bare mine sweep of thick lashes consumes
outrages that nest like worms in my blood,
and swim blind through my body's armored gates.
A car shouts its name from the distance, and
rolls through our dangerous sliver of dusk,
while you stand unmoved by steel distraction,
in silence, skin burned by polished debris,
then turn into the arc of my arms where
my hands crochet spider silk for your wounds,
and shape moonlight from the window into
a frieze of spears beneath bloody fingers.
I kneel to Jesus in a pool of piss,
shrieking through autumn's congealing music,
speaking tongues, fragrant baptism, and blues.

A. K. TONEY

In the Twilight

Suga, come give sum rhythm to a mac who's all 'dat
i mean, what up wit' me and u baby? Yo' lemme tell u what goes
on . . .
a look like yours is phat, tends to move a nigga's hustle
in a smooth sidestep swing
i mean, the way u move yo' hips makes me hop and i reminisce fo'
a future wit' a sistuh like u.
Ya-c, u're like chocolate clay sweetened wit' honey
and if a brotha like me could interlude inside yo'
indigo body . . .
'cuz in the ghetto u're a star but in my world u're the universe
i would float adrift on the space that hold those stars
so
twinkle
twila
twilight

Now what is a queen compared to yo' brightness
baby, u're like the bright light on the tip of a spliff, a nice twilight
high to calm the riff
a honeydip like u, could make a nigga like me, lose his realities
like poverty, suppression, and hustles of da' ghetto
positively baby, but maybe u could bring 'dis mac back
and make me better than 'dat.

the bridge
baby, bring me out on a bridge where our bodies can intertwine on a
chewy trip in bed
Ya-c, i wanna know what u feel 'cuz i know alone ain't nothin' but
long fo' us

to the bridge, where's the bridge away from my streets?
where sheets would be another door, befo' we went across, 'cuz
underneath would be another room. where the walls of covers
would glow, and more brightness would show. so suga, let yo' lil'
light shine.
but baby, bring me out on 'dat bridge underneath 'dat
twinkle
twila
twilight
of mine.
Now take a look at the dark heat we make caressing our insides
from the affection of silhouette strokes . . .
drippy-wet blus runnin'
down the skin of our blak bodies.
sweat blu
sweat blak
Suga u gotz body!
so don't hold back from 'dis mac
'cuz it's like soul electricity from our kindled close bodies
so let's combust blinding novas like a strobelite
while u
twinkle
twila
twilight.

JENOYNE ADAMS

Out-of-Body Experience

Compressed into a slither of the bed,
like sardines glad to share our millimeter of tin space,
we lie enraptured.

I peel my arm from your back and slip—
you didn't tell me I couldn't let go,
for a second,
to shake a cramp, yawn or turn over?

I didn't know your bed was a limb cast above rocks.

When I met you, I shouted, "Glory!" and joined you
on this mountaintop.

But now that I'm free-falling downward, I see the danger.

I see how the pattern of your spirit and the pattern set in the
palm of your hand and tattooed on the sides of my breast,
from when you cupped them tightly and held them up to God
like gifts you wasn't willing to give back,
I see how that pattern matches the granite and sedimentary below—
edge for edge.

How you get so high from depths so low?

I was so intoxicated by the crack of your ass,
that I found nourishment in your defecation, mistook your feces for a feast,
as you jungle-gym-fucked my mind & nigga-rigged my heart—

Open, long enough to steal me from myself
before I realized I was housed in an empty body.

And now that I lie here kissing rock,
with your purpose sprayed across my face like cheap cologne
that can't hide the smell of a late night, strobelight trick,

Now I feel the pangs of my emotions landing in the delta of my back from
    on high.

Only my emotions you throw back,
like bad fish to bubble and crack from exposure.
  Only my emotions you throw back.

Everything else you are keeping because I hear the splash of you bathing in
  my tears.

DJ RENEGADE

Hoodoo

Spell number one
      is the gingerbread brown
      splashing around in your eyes
Your San Diego smile
      slicing open like an orange
Your eyelashes curling
      into question marks
Spell number two is your voice
      spilling down my spine
      like a runaway tongue
The feather of your breath
      brushing my neck
Your fingertips skating
      across the skin of my chest
Spell number three is your name
      how it slips between my lips
      like a nipple
Softening into syllables
      that collect in the corners
      of my puckered mouth.

Touch Her

*To all the women
whose beauty and charm
has caused me to stutter.*

There's a woman who, when she's not around, causes my mind to
ramble through a cluttered archive of cute, charming,
compassionate, and conscious conversation to share.
Yet when we're in each other's face, my thoughts stumble over my
tongue clumsily falling from my lips an embarrassing example of
inarticulation.

But if I could just touch her

and yes I do mean with wise hands
soft and strong
that speak affectionately
to clothed or bare shoulders
that coerce tension to flee
when ceremony and smooth exotic oils
I baptize her in
soothing attention especially given
to that portion of her mid back
where erotic thoughts hide tickle and coo
given to the place where inner thighs
kiss lower cheeks
each other and my lips
commission these perceptive hands
to inquire of
unearth and scholarship
unexplored joys
the world her body

has long sheltered
nurture them all
never allowing contentment to stifle
discovery's need for more

yet how could the age of satisfaction
usher in its complete harvest
if I'm allowed only to caress her silhouette

if I could just
run my fingers through her wondrous imagination
hush her fears with the healing balm of my security
gently glide my care down the seams of her constitution
then leap into the skies of her continence
flapping my wings to blow away
storm clouds
hurtful secrets
and people who brought despair

if I could
stroke her with my breath made sweet by licorice
wild violets and a thirst for adjoinment

breeze across her cheek when I whisper
above the intonation of crowded rooms
the resonance of crowded memories
ancient tribal rhythms
coded conversation and my need
to identify just how to attach my warmth
to her chill bumps
melting everyone with a certain stare

console her with these whispering wind songs
seeping through the open windows of her essence
searching and finding her reclining spirit

to sweetly invigorate
with the sustenance that swims beneath my skin
the only place where fire and water mix without steam
where wind and earth mix with water and fire
to create tornado passions
the colors purple and blue
autumn breezes
and angels with brown hair eye and skin

if I could converse intimately with her purpose for living
coincide with her prayers for strength and kindness
deep french-kiss her hopes for eternity
suckle her need to be understood
have intercourse with her faith and focus
lick the hearty nectar tracing down the sides of her bitten
fruit
impregnate her with a solidifying notion of loving
support her high on a tower of adornment
standing with her proudly holding her hand

if I could just touch her
if I could just touch her
if I could just touch her

yea . . .

SHONDA BUCHANAN

Prayer

centaurian smoke blower
shyly smoking my breast
caught like a feather
in my dust

spare some fire for me
and i will swell
like the hickory
of wine in winter

sprawled on the quartz
of time
i
have heard your black
tongue picking the dance
from my wait
planting wheat in my scalp
mending whisper
into my eye
i come with a mark
on my back
drinking the music of
your breath
in staccato

MICHAEL DATCHER

i am open

(jenoyne's poem)

I.

walking backwards along shore
foraging for woman answers.
surveying where i have been
where i may return.
cross-examining scattered cowrie shells

remains of receding waves.
they woman spirit
compressed into sea stone by osun
for whispering sweet water secrets.

gather seven shells to ear
they afraid to speak.
pounce on nosy seagull
try to pry insight from beak
with long wisdom prayers.
she breaks silence
only after i promise to go down.
she comes mystic shaman tongues
pausing finally to moan:
what comes around goes around
what comes around goes around,
death chant of progressive macks
urbane snakes who wear goatees
heavy hearts on sleeves.
i am open.
come woman
come woman.
woman whose root doctor breasts
will strengthen spines of my warrior sons
whose seraphic light spirit
will show them god.
woman see me weep waterfall tears
when i cannot write.
see me electric stutter, skipping cd
not glance away.
woman whose third eye expose my cowardice
whose assata courage inspire my change.

woman who be truth.

come woman
come woman.
woman who love to fuck on stove top
like crisco smoking, popping, in black skillet
who make love like morning mist
caressing african violet.
who know my scorching sunstar heart sincere
even when salt in peanut gallery doubt me.
woman know i'm afraid of my dreams
call me "punk"
when cave to fear.
woman big lip, french kiss my mind
get sticky wet reading fanon
carry secret anhk shaped vibrator
inside bulging metu neter
sees beauty in farrakhan.
come woman
come woman.
woman say "motherfucker"
with gospel conviction, seven languages
then conjugate.
woman make me smile,
come woman
come woman.
woman know god a black woman
woman sense enough to worship herself.
who keep my nose open
like fifth street dick's
on south central, summer solstice nights.
who perry masons my nigga/nationalist contradictions.
woman let me lick her
like never ending roll, jelly roll morton, 32 cent stamps.
woman serious 'bout her people.
woman with low hanging

speed bump ass, no speed limit.
woman who can suck some dick.
woman know love oxygen of soul, water of spirit.
come woman
come woman.
woman black love her momma monk deep
got down home, home training.
woman fullmoon, barefoot, damballah dance
to crackling vinyl coltrane.

woman know god.

come woman
come woman.

nigrescent sherlock holmes
sandals, egyptian musk
mystery solving along shore.
searching for soul mate clues
praying waves wash up
cowries in hieroglyphic formation
ocean divination
prophesying my love story.

II.

we stand meditating on this beach
where i use to meditate alone.
sun at my back, casting cosby family fantasies
across the sea like a martinique fisherman
hurling his heavy net
starboard into a salty wind.
i called to the ocean.
you appeared hightide, a sunday morning.
pacific seashells rushing across my naked toes.
it was the matterhorn shaped one

pearl and orange colored.
you were curled inside, fetal position
like an early term black butterfly diva
waiting impatiently for her wings.
when you flew out
my heart was slow to recognize your beauty
like picasso with down syndrome.
i had you all wrong.
didn't see virgil adams chanting
on the front porch of your mind
girl make your daddy proud
girl make your daddy proud.

i prayed for you in a picket fence poem
come woman be my wife, come woman be my wife.

you are gazelle graceful.
handle struggle like george gervin finger roll.
pay the car note, gas bill, rent
one arm tied behind your back
the other testifying to god.
you are warrior
lionheart will accompany your name.
i see you on my mental canvas.
gardenia in your hair from billi's casket.
her gift to you:
a reminder that love does see color.
sometimes it is blue
like the man you have chosen.
i pick sunflowers from the sky.
your name and other mysteries
stenciled on the stems:
hieroglyphic ebonics for black lovers.
we are red hibiscus liberated from
oakland's jack london square

by a poor poet
who cannot afford the florist.
at sunbreak you open yourself to me
like the purple morning glories in my yard.
you let me be the sun
even when i bring the weight of
my heavy shadows across your face.

i prayed for you in a picket fence poem
come woman be my wife, come woman be my wife.

we have been through so much so soon.
we are the premature child born in winter
cold winds hitting our hearts
before the protection of spring.
bills trail us like home invasion robbers.
they know where we live.
you know all my fears.
i share them as if you're my bathroom mirror
my former closest confidante.
even when my sky is a blue note album cover
your smile streaks across it
like a dc 10 zooming above inglewood palmtrees,
you are the bruised blue jay cautious of bad weather
leaping from your nest into my storm
chancing being wounded in the house of a friend.

i walk among wolves for a living
selling ideas to the other world stage
that does not love me.
religiously i fall on my knees in desperate prayer
to barter myself, highest bidder
to people who'd slit my throat
if the light was right.

i lay on a bed of sharpened uniball pens
trying to sleep as my dream hangs by its ankles
out a 12th floor manhattan highrise window.
sometimes the wine color of my glasses
leaves my vision stumbling.
i'm so busy looking for god in people
i miss the bright yellow
diamond-shaped street signs
hanging from their necks that caution
devil straight ahead.
you recognize beelzebub when you see him.
you got my front and my back.

i prayed for you in a picket fence poem
come woman be my wife, come woman be my wife.

i sit in cafes meditating
my palms up, searching for truth between breaths
seeing the future, no crystal ball.
even the seer needs someone to see for him
when his eyes are clouded by doubt.
i need you to believe in me.

watching you sleep
is like sneaking up on the sun
napping behind kilimanjaro.
your body is a raw pine music box
i open and wind you up.
a siren song keeps me from straying
like the cat i am.
you smile at me in the morning
breasts still sensitive
from the intensity of my late night touch.
i smell your melody in my goatee.

you have become a romare bearden collage.
you're the faded photo of ella and diz
in front of birdland
torn from an old *downbeat* magazine.
you're a piece of chewed, tattered licorice root
found in the back seat
of a 1977 red and white cadillac
gangsta white walls.
you're the salt in betty's tears
the day before malcolm fell.
you're the cotton balls stuffed
in point of ballerina toe shoes
you never wore.
you're the crashing waves in the bathtub
filled with every storm
you couldn't stop with a prayer.
you're a page torn from the book of psalms.

you join my gemini i and i and i
with your aries hoodoo.
alone i am an out of key sextet.
together we are the duke ellington orchestra
live at the 1955 monterey jazz festival
blowing through caravan.
for our screaming encore
we appear as ourselves, naked before thousands
making love
dripping the sweaty bassline of coltrane's *olé*
from our vibrating bodies onto the wooden stage.
we levitate above jagged cliffs, no net, no parachute
we are holding on to each other's prayers
wind in our face like the peppermint breath of god
blowing kisses clothed in jet streams pushing us east.

some say i'm hard to please
say i don't know what i want.

they are wrong.
i know exactly what i want.
everything.
i have found that in you.
i see us standing naked on the beach
our dreams sandwiched in our embrace.
we are our own holy trinity
praying the horizon glows
in the crevice of our first son's smile.
i look into your eyes
see my grandchildren sitting around your skirt, asking
nana read us a poem.

i prayed for you in a picket fence poem
come woman be my wife, come woman be my wife.

KUPENDA AUSET (JOETTE HARLAND WATTS)

That Was Then

i remember that time
when you said
i was a good woman
that is when you usta
take me out to dinner
and hold the door for me
and make sure you were
on the outer side of the
sidewalk to protect me
and
that is when
you made sure

i wasn't going to
step in that mud puddle

that is when we
was vibing at the
Culture Center
with Jawanza and nem'

that was when you
couldn't stop smiling
at me

that was when you
introduced me to
Alizé and we listened
to the Blue Lights in the
Basement House Party

that's when you
spent the
night although we
didn't do anything

now
a month has passed and
i don't see you
now
i hear from you
every 3 days
this time it
was a whole week
now you are vague
and never available
you always have something
to do these days

now we can't never
have a decent phone
conversation when you
call me cause
you always got to answer
somebody's page, somebody's
call, somebody's anything
really

you said i was a
good woman
but that was then
now i am wondering
how you treat
the women who aren't
good.

DERRICK X (a.k.a. GOLDIE THE POET)

Shot to the Curb

Shot me to the curb
Left a brotha's ego in ruins
Couldn't comprehend her winter rejection
Stood her ground
Looked straight into baby bronze eyes and said no
Got me scrambling through the macking rule book
Searching for a proper comeback
But it's no use
Cause she meant that shit
Shot to the curb
Feeling like the game is inadequate
Need to reevaluate

Maybe the doctrine was too dogmatic
Cause baby took a sledgehammer to arrogance
A rebuff incisive enough to dispirit Jesus
Vetoes like some pitiful proposal
Impeached like a played-out politician
Stripped me of the airs that a player is known to flaunt
Then she rolled her piercing scissor eyes and slit me wide open
Revealing the bullshit
And I just stood there
Shot to the curb
And my ego is in ruins

CHERYL BOYCE TAYLOR

English Lace

Three hours have passed
without a ring of the telephone
a knock at my door
twice tonight i thought i saw you
pass under the street lamp
pink feather in your mouth

my left hand rubs the small swell
of my tummy my nipples harden
after a long blue summer
your touch is a broken shell
dried through with sun

i make the bed with english lace
cook curried eggplant
braid my hair girlish
with red beads and cowrie shells

hike up my white skirt
cut my lips
let blood flow like memory
like all things we've already lost.

DURIEL E. HARRIS

But There Are Miles

I am in a quiet place
leaves bunched in audience at my window
their deep green shapes shades of the night's stillness
I pause and consider
how different things could be

but there are miles, fitful
with no respect for persons
whole states, an expanse of mountains
uncharted geography of fear and doubt
grief

and you, lover
sigh in the pensive arms of sleep
in a separate peace
with one lank thigh languid over the other
your lips fallen open against her flesh
your features lost, nestled
in the soft spread of her breasts

our lovemaking was always tentative, hurried, desperate
jammed into the small space of days
and even when we lay together
our dreams were anxious wanderings

the bedcovers disheveled and damp with perspiration
the tense muscle of need a chasm between us

I am in a quiet place
my fingers trace the pattern of books strewn purposefully
on the other side of the bed

what I miss most is the slow sound of your breath
its slant rhythm

and your body
unfolded against mine
in rest

KYSHA N. BROWN

Brown Girl Blues

i had imagined you
brown to the bone

mahogany lifeblood
moving through your veins

and i really liked brown-black
boys with chestnut hands

even your nails
were brownish tan

you had to be
brown to the bone

i dreamt purple passion
and private pleasures

received them as gifts
in our daylight realities

exploding into crimson cries
for more always more

curiosity craved delight

then came that dark morning
like a black-hole horror-movie matinee

my eyes raging red, emotional sirens ablaze
floodlighting your infidelity

i tried to flee the scene of your crime
but you followed in pitiful pursuit

trapped in an elevator
we went low-down dirty
down seven floors to hell
f—— you, f—— her

and f—— both you muthaf——s
for f——ing each other

"listen to me"
   no
"let me talk to you"
   hell no

my eyes had heard
all you had to say

sunlight shining on that shit
you wanted to pass off as an apology

i hurried to my car
one hand holding my heart in place

the other searching for the key to freedom
in the bottom of my book bag

you shrank to nothing
on my heart's horizon

shrank to nothing
in my rearview mirror

i tried to drive my car into infinity

the car was runnin' fine
but i was singin' the broke-down blues

drivin' up this highway, and i'm feelin' might low
drivin' up this highway, sho nuff feel down and low
i just saw my man, under covers with his ho'

stomach wrenched
    heart moaned
        nostrils flared
            my eyes cried
                the brokenhearted
                    brown girl
                        blues

I Was Looking at Miles

Keith, the white man who lived
next door, invited me over
to see Miles Davis on the color
TV and then Keith started talking
in the middle of "Autumn Leaves."
Keith had read in a medical journal
that black men are bigger and in the case
does size really matter?
I was looking at Miles
on that horn, his face fracturing
in ecstasy and I wondered
if I should tell Keith that I don't hold
a thing against pale men or their bodies.
I don't think that I am racist, at least
I am not politically opposed to loving.
I wondered if I should be nice
to Keith who was giving me more
than a night's worth of entertainment
but I was looking at Miles
and I told Keith that I couldn't love
a man who couldn't make me blow
a note as sweet and high
as Miles just did.

Curious White Boy

Politically erect, romanticizing about ancestral innocence
Conscience easing, curiosity pleasing, slum teasing
Lab rat is crude ego food, ain't no afro nor halo
Can pick the cotton out your conscience
Inside the petting zoo
Was it good for you
Can't hide me in dark night places, cause in the spaces
Curious is the luxury to be wrong
White wrong still belong
All my jungle come out.
Curious white boy when am I gonna meet yo mama
Met yo daddy already
Another housekeeper fantasy
Afrodite
Coffee-colored remedy for yo hangover from history
I know your daddy and your brothers too well
And his friends made me swear I wouldn't tell
What you so mad about?
Always gotta scream and shout
Find a difference point it out
Spread your legs shut your mouth
My virginity hanging from your family tree
Why you so angry?
They just crowned mammy Miss America
Isn't she lovely

My Woman

Now what I can't understand is your plan to leave me be . . .
After years of trying to change your man
. . . all the sudden you claim you can't understand me?
Well, I don't understand you
but that don't mean that we're through
All the shit you done said to me,
Imagine if I flipped the script and pulled that same bullshit on you?
I don't feel like coming over tonight
so that means I don't love you?
I want to stay home alone and chill tonight
(Oh, so I *must* have another bitch coming over . . .)
I want to hang with my boys tonight
So that means I love them more than I love you . . . ?
Now if you know insecurity is the key to the start
of a bad relationship and a broken heart
then the fault is on whose part?
The things for which you hate me now
you loved back then
You don't like my style
so I try to be more . . . tasteful
While you continue to paint the picture of me as unfaithful
You hate that I'm a flirt
but you were attracted to that when we first met
And now you're so damned worried about me pursuing outside "wet"
Meanwhile, I'm turning down "wet" to the right of me,
turning away "wet," to the left of me,
saying no to "wet," right behind me,
and even refusing the "wet" in front of me . . .
See

the quantity of wet don't make it no party
All that "wet" don't mean a goddamn thing
cuz it *ain't* in the middle of your body!
BUT YOU CAN'T SEE THAT!!!!
. . . and now you want to let me go . . .
Remember when I would say, "Don't force it if it don't fit?"
"If You Love Somebody Set Them Free" . . . nah baby, that's bullshit . . .
If you love me then trust me in that I won't do you wrong
cause that song you sing in this game can only bring back the pain
of another lover's name
Deal with me cuz I'm a different type of nigga
I'm a 90s nigga
Look and you will find that in this day and time
I protect what's mine
So stop preparing for when I get caught out there
cuz that time will never come
But let me remind you, baby:
Don't start none won't be none

GLENN JOSHUA

On the Morning St. Bernard

pullin' up to the stop pullin' up to the stop aw man god please . . .

let her be there

basin street and canal
people gettin' on the bus
roodipoo hardlegs . . . a buncha old folks and a few mo' kids

two lovers . . . and there
there she is . . . up there paying her bus fare!

my daydream
my nightdream
my sweet drum machine thumpin' my heart in my throat, oh
come on sit by me! (I move my knapsack . . .
This seat's reserved, hack . . .)

and she does
the bus makes a right turn onto canal street headed for claiborne
and i'm captivated by a soft scent
softness, her hands and fingers unwrap a wine candy
(soft) i've got to say something this time
just "good morning," intelligent and polite so she can know
that my intentions are pure, honest, no time to waste . . .
gettin' close to cohen's tuxedo shop at the red light.

I glance her way
she's reading toni morrison while sucking on
watermelon-flavored contentment, like the weeks i've felt since I
first saw her
she is beautiful and black and smells so doggone good
she's a mcdonough #35 senior I could tongue-kiss till my lips explode
but I hesitate and hold still.

the bus nears kerlerec street and I know what that means
say something . . . tell her something, fool!
(the bus starts to stop) anything . . . (slower)
she begins to collect her things.

"you're sitting on my coat," she tells me
"oh . . ." I reply, "sorry"
she glances at the sticker taped on my three-ring binder
"st. augustine's? I guess you *are* sorry . . ."

the bus door opens
she's gone
I turn to look out the window
she's walking up the street, but not before looking back to the bus
searching, then finding me
she offers a sweet smile that immediately releases my butterflies and desires,
as if flung from a slingshot.

I return the favor with a waving finger and she knows i'll get a chance for
my rebuttal tomorrow.

because i've got her schedule down pat
the morning st. bernard, complete with watermelon wine candy,
good reading, and cherry-chocolate delights in eyes that are soft . . .
so soft . . .

next day the bus pullin' up to basin street and canal.

"naw, man . . . I ain't movin' my knapsack . . .
this seat's reserved, jack . . ."

LISA B. THOMPSON

What Do I Want from Men and Love?

I walk down the aisles of my local video store
maybe he'll be standing there
a Black African Caribbean Afro American West Indian man warrior
tall lean, short stocky stout, muscles tense, loose overweight
glasses contacts vision 20/20
dark light medium red bone tone
smiles or concentrated frown
balding fade dreads

preppy hip-hop gangsta
sandals loafers sneakers doc boots
east coast homeboy west coast square
bicoastal bisexual southern fried tender
multitongued monolingual
poet podiatrist plumber
mama's boy or child of foster care
friend father free
with no sista waiting at home
a brotha, outward manifestation or representation not withstanding.

His face I expect is buried in the foreign films
trying desperately for the last time to find *Sugar Cane Alley*
struggling to keep Cornel's *Prophetic Fragments*
from spilling on the floor at his feet
He is looking for me
a dreadlock sista queen
drinking Evian and whispering to myself among the documentaries
a tattered copy of *Maud Martha*
bulging from a weathered black leather backpack
walkwoman blasting Wayne Shorter's brass reed pleas.

We are both lonely for
new sweet memories of
tender-whispered hunger redefined
and glad stomping on the floors of sensual sanctuary.
We want slow Sunday mornings
wrapped in ivory sheets and heat.
Our desires for simple sin, bathing at midnight
and tears as a way to forgive
will bring us the harmony of friendship.
A commitment to sharing
danger, laughter, and pecan pie
draws us into love.

His name will dance upon my lips
Adam Alan
Bill Blair
Charles Chad
Dexter Darryl Elijah Ernest
Freddie Frank
Gerald Hakeem Ian
Jordan Jamal
Lawrence Lance lover
Lover,
are you there?

And he will answer yes
from the office studio study
as I sit in the sunken living room of our
two bedroom plus den
with hardwood floors, lots of light
a working fireplace, service porch, formal dining room
and french doors overlooking a patio
with the sounds of the ocean or busy city
floating into our bathroom with original aqua blue tile
and enough room to dry my
100% cotton panties next to his political T-shirts
that we share with our books and CDs while saving enough money
for a dream home with space enough for babies
with nappy hair and attitudes.

Until then I find my film movie video
pick up some Thai takeout and go home.

Everyday

Hook:
Everyday I need my shit done in a special way . . . Everyday

Off the top niggas see me and want to serve
Just thinking about what they need
Ain't that some nerve
Now look at here 24 hours and
7 whole days, I demand my respect
I demand my praise,
Everyday that I wake
I gotta have everything done with no mistakes
I take it incredibly slow so don't try to rush me
No means no, I never said a no that meant yes
Other women get taken for granted—I guess
I got a wish list that must be fulfilled
And you gets none until I get my toes sucked
And my eyebrows plucked
I need my car waxed and my floor shellac
I need my back rubbed and da bubbles in the tub
that float me to the bed so that we can make love

Hook:
Everyday I need my shit done in a special way
Everyday I need my shit done in a special way

It ain't much to ask for when
I come off tour to have my truck washed
Or my body massaged
All the bills paid
I send home all my dough
And you being my man, it just ain't for show

139

All the lovey dovey yeah that is sweet
but honey bunny you gotta earn your keep

But don't sleep cause I need a lot of shit done
So get started
Call me cold harded yeah check it out
Whatever is clever
And get to stepping if you know something better
if not then respect what'cha got
Meanwhile I got a new ride at the lot
Pick it up and bring it back to the spot
This is how we do it now everyday
I need it done a special way, baby
Tell them how it goes

Hook:
Everyday I need my shit done in a special way
Everyday I need my shit done in a special way

On the real I need a man that understands me and
realizes the reality I'm in the M.C. Industry which
means if I want to live lovely, I gotta make money
Listen so never ask me to give it less than what I got
If it's too hot nigga then raise up out my spot
It's my trade I made up the black ace of spade
Alone in the world but it's me ya can't fade
It's my life, I do it my way
You don't like my way, hit the highway
See I'm special not because I'm MC Lyte, but
because I'm a woman with the gift to bear life, it's
    done
Yes I've rested my case now run pick up my
    dermalogica
for my face

This is how it goes down everyday
I need it done in a special way, baby

Hook:
Everyday I need my shit done in a special way
Everyday I need my shit done in a special way

OJENKE

Amazon

She who dances in campfire flames
She who laughs at wolf calls
She who dashes thru uncharted places
like a roadrunner
She who slashes the air with her rhythmic body
She who raises earth dust with primitive foot stomping
She who has a forest fire in her rump
She who is as slender and graceful as river stalks
She who has a rasta head of hemp locks
She who has a wild exotic flower
rooted at the vertex of her thighs
She who wears necklaces of tiger teeth
She who pirouettes on elephant tusks
She who liberated her body from the clothes of city women
and is black beautiful beaming in the night of fireflies
She who is as sophisticated as the river Niger
She who listens to the wind then argues
with nature killers and butterfly hunters
She was named by salamanders
She who laid down by the still waters of the Lord
and grew big-bellied

She who slept on the dark side of the moon
and rose up in the valley of death eating silver cheese
She who caresses the acupuncture points of pleasure
She who left the metropolis of boody fuckers
and tired-dick businessmen
She who is the lover of stormy lovers
She wears the scarlet letter on her forehead like a crown
She reconciles the palpitating flesh spears of warriors
She who has a black body ornated with battle scars
amorous scratching
She who climaxes like aurora borealis
She who is a punk prover and
a man testifier

She who never bullshits
She who I am seeking among the marble-hipped women
whose wombs only give forth second-rate tobacco
She who is a flower dancing alone in an uncharted forest
She who is woman au natural

Chapter 4

Revolutions

ABIODUN OYEWOLE (of The Last Poets)*

Derrick Gilbert A lot of folks have called The Last Poets the fathers of rap. Is this an accurate description?

Abiodun Oyewole Ironically, The Last Poets have been given this great, great honor of having been the progenitors of rap. That's very nice, but the fact is that we just popularized the word by putting it on wax in the late sixties and early seventies. We just helped to create a marketplace that introduced the industry cats to the spoken word.

DG A lot of your early poetry constantly used the word *revolution*. In fact, a lot of the poetry that came out during the late sixties and early seventies talked about *revolution*. But, today, we don't really see young poets writing about *revolution*—or at least they're not using the "R" word. What do you make of this changing dynamic?

AO I'm growing and evolving, and I think that revolution is something that comes with evolution. And in evolving, growing, and developing, I realized that I don't just want to destroy. You know, I don't just want to destroy—I don't want to destroy the Republican party, the Democratic party, and all the people who believe in that kind of system. No! I don't want to just destroy all the oppressive types of behavior that've been taking place in this land for so many years. I mean, to wipe that out would be wonderful on one hand, but what do we replace it with? It could be the same thing, because a lot of us only know what we've experienced and what

*This interview was conducted the day after the death of rapper Tupac Shakur.

we've been dealt—and this hand is not necessarily a winning hand no matter who's holding it. So, I've come to realize that in order to be a true revolutionary, I've got to be about something better than what is right now. I can't just be about disliking this; I've got to be about something I like—something I am really willing to promote, produce, and show as an example of change. That's where my world is now.

I'm looking at the fact that we were sacred people a long time ago—that we're beautiful, talented, gifted geniuses on the planet. We've always been in harmony with nature; we've brought that to the world. In whatever setting we've been in, we've always given something—and that's what I want to get back to. I want to understand that the gift we were given inherently from the beginning of time is something that we need to build on. Also, we need to stop looking at our life on the depravity level. Unfortunately, the prevailing systems are not designed to really praise the glory of us and our existence on this planet. So, we have got to deal with the systems that we've created—and poetry is an extraordinary system that we've created that really exalts us and puts us in high esteem when we are feeling good about ourselves. We need to take a look at the words and music we've created, and we need to take a look at all the creations that we have rendered on this planet and see how we can feed ourselves from the things that we've created for others. For example, we don't have jazz used in the schools—it's not used as a medicine. And when it is used, it's just looked upon as music, but it's more than that—it's science and math and much more. These type of things need to be exploited and explored more in a school setting.

We also need to begin looking more closely at rap music. You see, rap is more than just some loud ranting and raving—it's an expression of a people at a particular time based on what they have been handed. There's a certain type of cry for independence in it. You know, there are a lot of insights in everything that we've done creatively, but we're not really looking at them because we don't see the merit in it. So the whole concept of revolution to me is to endorse ourselves as who we are—as superhuman beings with a great heart, and a great generosity, and a great will that has allowed us to sustain ourselves in spite of the bad deals that we've been given. So the revolution is something like the inner development of self—recognizing that we've got to build something around ourselves to secure this belief in the inner self.

DG Can you elaborate on the current state of rap/hip-hop?

AO First of all, I have a lot of respect for the spoken word. I say that because I think that hip-hop is just another branch of that tree; I think it's part of a great history that we've always carried with us from day one. I've always seen hip-hop like bebop. In another words, hip-hop moves away from tradition and the dominating idiom of the moment and takes some chances with a new idiom—just like the bebop cats did. So rap is poetry, but it's poetry taken from another position. It's got poetic nuances—you know, it's got a lot of alliteration, metaphors, similes . . . it's got all this stuff happening. And it's got the prose, obviously, and the encasement is usually the rhyme. And that's all cool and fine—and I think it makes sense . . . and I think we have a lot to say with that idiom. "The Message" by Melle Mell is a classic example of what we can say to motivate and make people think. "Keep Your Head Up" by Tupac is another very important inspirational piece.

DG Given your last reference, what do you think about the death of Tupac Shakur?

AO With the Tupac thing I know some kids are going to say: "Well, if you play in the traffic, you're going to get hit." That's how many of us will view it—it's just a nonchalant view of life. And Tupac will be glorified by some kids—somewhat like Jimmy Dean for white boys. You know, Jimmy Dean was a rebel without a cause and Tupac was a rebel without a cause. Tupac really didn't represent a cause—other than the public madness between the two industries: the left coast and the beast coast, as far as I'm concerned.

There's nothing really that serious that we should be fighting over, because none of it is ours. In fact, the game is not even ours to determine. So it's sad right now, but I think that hip-hop is in a strategic place because it has the ears of a lot of our young people today. Hip-hop can still make the strongest impact among the youth, and I think it can be a very strong instrument to change a lot of the negative attitudes and the negative activities that have been taking place under the heading of hip-hop. I think hip-hop can actually transform itself into something much greater and much more productive than what it is. But right now it's in the confusement park more than it is in the amusement park—it's kind of sad in many ways.

DG With that, what would be your advice to the rappers and young poets today?

AO Well, write from your heart and from your experience. Don't always cry about the misfortunes of life, because that seems to be something we're always willing and able to blurt out. But try to find a solution. Try to offer something more than the pain, because we're overwrought with pain and grief—and it's not really helping us. I would like to see the writing become more healing; I would like us to become more conscious about what we say to each other—with the hope that we can help each other instead of tearing each other down.

DG How do you want The Last Poets to be remembered?

AO I would like, first of all, for people to realize that we really took the idea of writing poetry seriously—that we were true craftsmen of that particular genre. I want people to know that we took the whole concept of writing seriously; I want people to know that we didn't just write garbage. I also want our writings to be meaningful outside of the time context in which they were written; I'd like to know that what we've said will last forever. I just hope that when it all goes down, that the poetry of The Last Poets, and that my personal poetry, were examples of tremendous growth in a society that did not want any of us to grow.

ABIODUN OYEWOLE

When the Revolution Comes

When the revolution comes
some of us will catch it on TV
with chicken hanging from our mouths
you'll know it's revolution
because there won't be no commercials
when the revolution comes
preacher pimps are gonna split the scene
with the communion wine stuck in their back pockets
faggots won't be so funny then
and all the junkies will quit their nodding
and wake up
when the revolution comes
transit cops will be crushed
by the trains after losing their guns
blood will run through the streets of Harlem
drowning anything without substance
when the revolution comes
Revolution is silent
I hope pearly-white teeth fall out of the mouths
that speak of revolution without reference
the course of revolution is 360 degrees
understand the cycle that never ends
understand the beginning to be the end
and nothing in between but space and time
that I make or you make to relate or not to relate
to this world outside my mind your mind
speak not of revolution until
you are willing to eat rats to survive
when the revolution comes
when the revolution comes

Black cultural centers will be forts
supplying the revolutionaries with food and arms
white death will fall off the walls
of museums and churches
breaking the lie that enslaved our mothers
when the revolution comes
jesus christ is gonna be standing
on the corner of Malcolm X Blvd. and 125st
trying to catch the first gypsy cab out of Harlem
when the revolution comes
afros will be straightening their heads
and straightened heads are gonna be
trying to get afros
when the revolution comes
women are gonna look like women
and men are gonna look like men again
when the revolution comes
but until then you know and I know
niggers will party and bullshit and party and bullshit
and party and bullshit and party and bullshit and party
and some might even die
before the revolution comes

MARIO VAN PEEBLES

To Hell with Whitey
(*From the movie* Panther)

Whitey drops Napalm on the Yellow man
Slaughters and betrays the Red man
Enslaves and mutilates the Black man
An' fucks with anyone else he can

An' damn
Whitey even messes with
The birds
The trees
An' the fish swimmin' in the sea
'Cause whitey can't see
That
If he messes with Mother Nature
Mother Nature will mess with whitey
But damn
Some of us can't see
'Cause we're too busy tryin' to be
Just like mister whitey
But dig it, y'all
That ain't right
'Cause whitey ain't right
An' it ain't right
To wanna be white
But what is right
Is to get all that white
Out of you
An' to get all that white
Out of whitey
Too
'Cause brothas and sistahs
Can't you tell
If we follow whitey
We'll ALL go to hell!!!

CHUCK D

But Can You Kill the Nigga in You?

Chorus
Now you wanna kill me
that may be true 1,2
cause my lyrics be true
but can you kill the nigga in you

Verse I
quiet as it's kept
some of y'all slept on yourself
next time you hit the mirror black
turn your back on yourself
I wouldn't trust some a y'all
if you was my right hand, man
I'd cut it off at the wrist
like your name was Benedict
enough lead
to threaten 50 niggas dead, you said
cause niggas is back to perms & relaxers
all up in their head
TV niggas only make you laugh, embarrass
can u catch it
nigga fever new season
of modern-day Stepin Fetchits 1990s'
niggas be 'fraid of the noise I made
'bout their master crackers giving out disasters in the
    hood
phony honeys be gone when they moneys be gone
niggaresses artificial chests'
posin fake hair & high dresses

Chorus
Now you wanna kill me
that may be true 1,2
because my lyrics be true
but can you kill the nigga in you

Verse II
Madd niggas hittin shit
but they health be quittin it
clothes and car makin the men
havin counterfeitin fit
seizing niggas be praisin
Benzes Beemers when they got em
shined and simonized foreclosed
bit they grilles be rotten
Simon sez niggas jump
and they jump for these Hilfigers Tommy hates
Niggas high-priced styles
white as wild rice
niggas be dwellin in hell and the
negroes pray for heaven
fuck the preacher he don't reach
yo my nigga roll a seven

niggas forgettin trips about those slavery ships
niggas wasn't there they claim
fuck that nigga bring the pain

niggas be dealin Narcotic
but don't get the money nigga
women or the fame my nigga
or the muthafuckin game

Chorus
Now you wanna kill me
that may be true 1,2
cause my lyrics be true
But can you kill the nigga in you

ROLAND POET X

The Divided States of America

I asked for a father on Father's Day,
a mother on Mother's Day,
a sister that wasn't an orphan,
a brother that wasn't abandoned/
I got no job on Labor Day,
no Thanks for Giving Day.
I didn't get shit for Christmas,
but an empty box full of broken promises,
unfulfilled proclamations
IOUs a mule, 40 acres, and reparations.

I didn't get Freedom on Independence Day,
I got a warrant for my arrest,
a battering ram on my front door,
a shotgun breaking my windows,
an ungodly voice in a cloud of tear gas:
COME OUT! HANDS BEHIND HEAD! LEGS SPREAD!

Then I'm surrounded by the Gestapo,
The Fascist Bureau of Investigation,
The S-S-Secret Service,
for threatening to kill the President
and all his cronies in Congress

spending billions on the Military
while cutting welfare for millions of children,
sealing their futures as hardened criminals.

And I'm kicked like a stray dog in America,
refusing to bow down to a Master,
go fetch his daily propaganda,
to roll over and play dead,
even though clubs bash my hard head,
as brothers and sisters in dashikis look on,
raising their voices but not a helping hand,
while pimps and drug dealers mock a prophet,
as they make a profit:
Putting their own race into boxcars,
wrapping them up in barbed wire,
pulling gold out their mouths,
tattooing arms with needle marks,
stripping their dignity in the showers
of sweat and tears that become poison,
crack cocaine and heroin,
making it easier for the ovens,
turning neighborhoods into crematoriums,
Black Power into Genocide.

What We Got Here Is *My* Failure to Communicate . . .

My failure to capitulate.
My failure to be blind to see,
deaf to hear, mute to speak.
My failure to forget my history,
even though it's déjà vu all over again,
the same ole song-'n-dance,
the same record stuck in an ill groove.
My failure to ignore where I came from:
A Black Slave raped by a White Master

creating a Brown Bastard that couldn't be a
House Nigger because he kept trying to burn it down,
and couldn't be a Field Nigger because
he kept throwing rocks instead of picking cotton.
My failure to buffoon for an Oscar,
sell my ass to go Platinum,
wave Old Glory for a Gold Medal,
cry when I win and whine when I lose.
My failure to vote in
another grifter in Congress,
another liar for President,
another adulterer in Camelot,
another actor that's a puppet.
My failure to move forward,
when I'm being held down by stormtroopers,
beaten into blackness:
Floating in the blood of the indigenous,
listening to screams in the distance,
from an empire though invincible,
christened with venom,
powered by capitalism,
driven to disaster by arrogance,
slowly sinking while the band's still playing
Olympic themes and National Anthems,
until everything is silent . . .
and I don't know if I'm dead or back in Solitary,
where manna came in through a slot in the dark,
and I threw shit back out.

Just waiting 400 years for a veil to be lifted,
muscles to contract,
a virgin's womb to be opened up . . .
And I'm born again as a Warrior,
with a sword to slay my enemies,
a gun to hunt them down,

a bomb to blow them apart,
a sinner that's a savior,
with apostles that learn to fight back,
not to turn their cheeks but strike one,
do twice unto the politicians,
using patriotism and religion,
to rob, rape, and murder.
In God They Lust,
In God They Corrupt,
In God They Conquer,
in the Divided States of America.

Revolution

Revolution (Refrain)
(Repeat)
Brothers and sisters (Refrain: Revolution)
Let me share with you some news
As I sit on my best couch watching the news
There has been a rude awakening
That I have marched until my feet have bled
And I have rioted until they called the feds
"What's left?" My conscience said
"What's left?" My conscience said (Revolution)
Go—As I look out my window I see the little ones
Playing amongst each other with the water guns—sit there in poverty
Generations of good people in cycles of poverty
It bothers me so I ask myself I say
Are you doing as much as you can for the struggle (No)
Am I doing as much as I can for the struggle (No)
Then why do I cry when my people are in trouble (Yo)

My ancestors slapped me in the face and said (Go)
Harriet Tubman told me to get on up
Marcus Garvey said to me brother ya' get on up
My brother Malcolm X—need I name more
It ain't like you never seen blood before
Come on let's talk Revolution, now (Revolution)
All my people say Revolution
All my brothers say Revolution
All my sisters say Revolution
All my people say Revolution
Hey—Revolution
All my people say—come on—Revolution
All my people say Revolution
I see blood I want Malcolm as my child
I see tears 'cause it almost seems that we forgot him
I seen years of people searchin' for solutions
Restitution—excuses—Don't want no more confusion
Come on—Come on—Let's talk right—Let's talk right
Talk up—Talk up, but don't talk up all night
There's got to be action if you want satisfaction
If not for yourself—for the young ones (the children)
The UN—The U.S. We can't allow ya' to tell us that gettin' together
was not as important as gettin' in Bosnia
I ain't with it (Uh-huh)—Just forget it (No)
You can't even debate it if you don't understand our situation (Come on)
You don't want us to go get a gun now, do ya
You don't like to see people runnin' around now
Yet still ya' wanna live like *90210* while we scream out (Yo) Freedom
My grandmothers are goin' we are wasted
You must acquire a taste for something never never tasted (Uh-huh)
So people let us wet our palates (Word)
It's either the bullet or the ballot—Go now
Revolution Now (Revolution)
All my people say (Revolution)
All my brothers say (Revolution)

All my sisters say (Revolution)
All my people say (Revolution)
Let's talk about a Revolution
All my people say (Come on)
Revolution
(Repeat)
Now see I understand what my people have said
It's havin' to fight
Fight for the ancestors who are dead
For Harriet Tubman—Move organization
David Watts—the Black Panthers—Kwame
Nkrumah—Marcus Garvey and Jane Pittman
Revolution (Refrain)
(Repeat)

OKTAVI

Pardon Me

Dear, Mother-Father God

When I die
I don't want
My stone to read
Black bump on the ass of America
I'm bringing a White-Water-Gate gangsta-gentlemen
Handpicked by the Senate Appropriations Committee
To my arraignment at the pearly gates
I want the kind of pardon that got
Dickie, Ronnie, and Ollie off

I have been indicted for
Dabbling in a few of the seven deadly sins

The S&L scandal was not my doing
There ain't no banks in my neighborhood and
I sure didn't enslave nobody or
Pump drugs and bullets into the veins of America
Didn't hose down the streets of Birmingham with Black bodies

I don't want St. Peter or the Press Corps thumbing through
Transgressions in my personal diaries
I want them sealed by the FBI
Stamped Top Secret
I want the guys with the business cards that read
We can cover-it-up
Cause God is on our side
To get me my pardon

Can't they make the book parchment
Thirsty for my name to be
Written in permanent, indelible ink
Cause if I'm not
Red, white, blue, star-spangled banner holy
When they finished
Then we should all
Be sitting around hell
The Freedom of Information act in hand
Digging up dirt on the folks that put us here

Don't Hate Me!

Don't hate me cause my skin is smooth like fine lustrous fiber forming a tuft
on an ear of Corn.
Don't scorn me
Cause my color is dark like the coat of a stallion, making you *hard* to
understand me.
I have secrets and mysterious ways that leave you in a state of ignorance,
But, don't hate me.
I don't hate you
Don't hate me
Cause the melanin in my skin protects me from Cancer,
And the spirit in the wind keeps me Strong,
And the rhythm in my works makes hit songs, but, please don't hate me.
Don't hate me cause I'm beautiful.
Don't dislike me cause your little boy cannot understand why you tell him not
to play with My little boy, why he can't see color, but see friend, and you're
angry at him for that. You're upset at me for that! You're enraged at me
cause of your own prejudice! And you hate me cause he goes out and plays
with him anyway!
Don't hate me.
And you want me to hate you . . . but I don't.
You want to justify your hatred with mine . . . but it won't.
Don't hate me.
I don't hate you.
I may talk about you, even ridicule you. I try to make you see things that you
don't.
But, I don't hate you . . .
And don't hate me,
Don't hate me cause
I'm beautiful.

Capitalism Is a Brutal Motherfucker

*uhmmmmmm somebody's tellin me
that I'm a worthless piece of
shit uhmmmmmm somebody's
tellin me that I'm a low-down
dirty dog uhmmmmmmm who
can it be who can it be that's
tellin me uhmmmmmmm*

*What do a 400-year-
old cracker cost?
What do a 400-year-
old cracker cost?
YOUR LIFE MOTHERFUCKER
YOUR LIFE!*

As-Salaam-Alaikuming
They keep bombing & napalming
We too busy As-Salaaming
& Alaikuming
While they bombing &
napalming
As-Salaam As-Salaam
As-Salaam-Alaikum
Shut the fuck up &
Pass me the bacon,
diet not gonna kill we, nah!
We be krypto nitro crippled back
twisted bedbug rage immune to what's been
going down, what bees going down
pouring down on we head
likes acid rain

for the brain
We eats poison
We likes poison
We Mikey
We eat anything
We old man w/ penniless pension
poot booty check for cisco & cognac
& cigarettes & beer
& LOTTO—don't forget the
LOTTO for your ass though you
pushin 70 w/ a bum leg & one
lung, gotta pay for that pacemaker,
white man charge you for
after he done fucked up your air,
whitey charge for everything
even coax you to get medicaid,
pocket money for the young bup bureaucratic
exploits,
poisoned & poisoning
poisoned & poisoning
full of the white man's lies
& doodoo, brownstone buppies lost
& fucked-up beleaguered snot-nosed dogs puppy poo
poo gibberish laid out on a bearskinned
parqueted floor, scratching & salivating
& panting, licking white hoes' legs,
Geraldo Rivera style
waiting for a new movie to define your
reality,
hooked up show me babies glued to
a tube, frosted flake new jack belly
ache, w/ big ass suitcases for earrings
& a 8-ball jacket bull's-eye
givin proof to the lie
givin price to the mind's eye,

the I in us, stamped out alone distorted
material worshipers
makin white cops' jobs easier
Behind the 8-ball,
little white cue ball on the 8-ball's ass
That's where they want us, Love
like the 8-ball,
rack em up jack em up
pushed aside,
sunk
in the corner pocket of extinction!
8 ball jacket full of shit shearling piece of
worthless crap—bull's-eye! bull's-eye!
I WANT I WANT I WANT bullshit
LIE Bullshit LIE
LAY DOWN & DIE I WANT
I WANT LAY DOWN LAY DOWN
New Jack Hustler, Sellout Rustler,
Constipated dead dreamer dreaming up
a new lie reality, dreaming up the
money
monger madness of material worship
& sellout lackey temptation
eat shit & die, eat shit & die
poisoned rabied cobwebbed flies,
stuck in the corner of the world, stuck
in the corner of a wall called America
land of the 6/10th of 1% rich & masses & masses
of poor oppressed hungry screaming ugly ass
woogies, wild hair snot & madness dizzy
w/ stomach growls & tears drowning in a cesspool
of fears,
whipped sho nuff qué pasa mommies,
show me some leg & thigh
O hot latin freak jigaboo for

Shearson Lehman, for IBM, for
Sears & Roebuck, for Anne Klein &
Heinz Ketchup, a new vegetable
to go w/ them fries you
sellin for mc donald's mc daddy's
mc boom boom & whip whip
Shut up slave!
& serve the motherfuckin dinner
after you scrub my bathroom
floor w/ your tongue!
After you wipe my mother's old
wrinkled flabby pale red dotted pruny
spotted ass,
after you take my baby
out for an afternoon stroll,
or would you rather be
back on that Island
hikin up your skirt for
us tourists?!!
show me baby show me baby
how you serve up some red meat
& cyanide show me
how you wipe that old bitch's ass
with sandpaper & itching powder
how you stroll that little white devil
wouldbe capitalist wouldbe racist
wouldbe exploiter & imperialist
into the Harlem River belly up w/
the dead fish & condoms
showed me baby show me how you
slit that white motherfucker's throat
how you tear that ofay's dick off w/
your teeth & serve it to him in his
soup!
Show me like that old wino jesus

showed me the other day on the
3 train going to Brooklyn, drunk &
stumbly rush w/ the wind show me
how like he showed me w/ his dancin
eyes & bloated feet yellin at nobody
& yellin at everybody: DON'T FUCK WITH ME
YOU 40-YEAR-OLD CRACKER! DON'T FUCK WITH ME
YOU AINT SHIT! YOU AINT SHIT!
And we hear you old man prophet warrior beaten down
booted out stomped on crushed back stubborn old
age rage, we hear you we hear you & we times
that 40 w/ 10 we be scientists we be mathematicians
we analyze and know that 40 × 10 is 400,
A 400-Year-Old Cracker Fuckin w/ our Head
& Livelihood,
A 400-year-old cracker called capitalism
& capitalism be on our ass
Capitalism be on
our ass like hot breath
of dogs snappin at
our fluttering
bleeding bowels
buried in the snow of
white supremacy & this
won't cleanse us & this
won't heal & save us
& Jesus won't save us
& Allah won't save us
The Pope w/ his big gold ring
in his souped-up cadillac pimp mobile
won't save us
Ten hundred Jehovah's Witnesses
selling the same magazine
won't save us &
humming Buddha motherfuckers

won't save us &
turbans & sandals & braids
& sheets & oils & candles &
perfume & shit won't save us
dances & jackets & earrings
& hairstyles & hairdos &
high-top fades & Nike sneakers &
Michael Jordan & nu-lie relaxed
Spike Lee flick won't save us
A club full of bumpin grindin boogalooing
woogies won't save us less we doin the
death dance on whitey's economic head
& the Young & the Restless won't save
us & big ass bourgeois Oprah & horse-
teeth Arsenio won't save us & half-Jew
Geraldo won't save us/not Elvis,
the new Jesus/not that dumb bitch
Barbara Walters & that constipated
motherfucker William Buckley & all the
dumb-ass weak shit that America has to offer
won't save us BUT US & SCIENCE &
MACHINE GUNS & HEART & LOVE
OF LIFE & LOVE OF PEOPLE & LOVE
FOR PEACE & LOVE & LOVE & LOVE
will save us
Revolution will save us
Revolution will save us
Revolution will save us

NADIR LASANA BOMANI

A Philosophical Perspective on Everyday Shit

i look at life like
milk of magnesia; white, thick
& hard to swallow.

EDDIE GRIFFIN

Mind of a Madman

Mind of a Madman kills
Mind of a Madman steals
Steals and kills the future
of Mankind, Hiskind because
he feels he out of time
Selfish beyond his discontent
So his soul has no content
2 him Love is a 4-letter word
Like, Fuck and Shit
yet he say I'm down wit it
Down 4 whatever whenever
So is the Devil
So 4 U soon I'll carry a shovel
Diggin more dirt
It don't hurt
It don't hurt
Desensitized 2 the power of God
until 6 pallbearers carry that rod
So our future goes down in the ground
Kings, queens, the cure 4 starvation

has been buried in this nation
Mind of a Madman steals kills
Mind of a Madman u have skills
Skills u use oh so well
Skills that are in hi demand in Hell
Mind of a MadmanNnNnNnnnNNNNN

ADWIN BROWN

Donut Man

the tones of the 60s vibrated
in my ears & the word was Revolution!
as a child i loved things that spin
coins   a top   a ball
& i knew i wuz gonna change things
make this world spin on my finger y'all
so i got educated
i could philosophize quote rousseau
cervantes gilbran emerson thoreau
i read quantum theory string theory
hell i read timothy leary but
along the way i lost the plan
i wuz well-rounded see
with no center

i wuz donut man

suddenly the only revolution i knew
wuz the rotation of the planet
livin day ta day ta day
stranded on a kiln

i wuz clay
oozing through the fingers
of everyone else's whims and ideas
of what i should be
molded and shaped like dough
never minding cuz it's cool

2b needed

one day i looked in the mirror
and didn't recognize the person staring back
next day it wuz the same way
& the day after that
there wuz a stranger hanging on the wall
so eventually
i stopped lookin at all

CRYSTAL A. WILLIAMS

In Search of Aunt Jemima

I have sailed the south rivers of China and prayed to hillside Buddhas.
I have lived in Salamanca, Cuernavaca, Misawa, and Madrid.
I have stood upon the anointed sands of Egypt and found my soul in their
                                                                        grains.
I am a global earth child who is still excluded from conversations on vacation
                                                                        hot spots.

I have read more fiction, nonfiction, biographies, poetry, magazines, essays,
                        and bullshit than imaginable, possible, or even practical.
I am beyond well-read and am somewhat of a bibliophile.
Still, I'm gawked at by white girls on subways who want to know why and
                                how I'm reading T. S. Eliot.

I have shopped Hong Kong and Bangkok out and sent them to replenish their
                                                                    stock
in heat so hot the trees were looking for shade—I was the hottest thing
                                                            around.
Still I'm followed in corner stores, grocery stores, any store.

I can issue you insults in German, Spanish, and some Japanese.
Still, I'm greeted by wannabe-hip white boys in half-assed ghettoese.

I've been 250 pounds, 150 pounds, and have lived and loved every pound
                                                        in between.
I am still restricted by Nell Carter images of me.

I've eaten rabbit in Rome, paella in Barcelona, couscous in Morocco,
and am seated at the worst table by mentally challenged maître d's who
                                think my big ass is there for coffee.

I am still passed up by cabs
passed over for jobs
ignored by politicians
guilty before innocent
Black before human.

I am still expected to know Snoop Dog's latest hit
Mike's latest scandal.
I am expected to believe in O. J.'s innocence.
And I am still expected to walk white babies up and down 92nd street as I
                                            nurse them, sing
a hymn and
dance a jig.

Sorry, not this sista, sista-girl, miss boo, miss it, miss thang, honey, honey-
                                                            child, girl
girlfriend.

171

See, I am not your militant right-on sista wearing dashikis and 'fros with my
fist in the air
spouting
Black Power while smoking weed, burning incense, and making love to
Shaka—formerly known as Tyrone.

I am not your high-yellow saditty college girl flaunting Gucci bags and
Armani suits
driving an alabaster-colored Beemer with tinted windows and A.K.A. symbols
rimming
my license
plate.

I am not your three-babies-by-fifteen, green dragon lady press-on nails welfare fraud ghetto
Ho
whose rambunctious ass is stuffed into too tight lycra with a lollipop hanging
out the side
of my mouf
and a piece of hair caught in a rubber band stuck to the top of my head.

I am not your timberland, tommy hilfiger, 10k hollow-hoop wearin
gangsta rappin
crack dealin
blunt smokin
bandana wearin
Bitch named Poochie.
And I am not your always supportive, constantly smiling, black-face sounding
board for your
obsessive whining about those democrats and decreased nra support.

I am not your conscience clearer.
I am not your convenient Black friend.
Notyourprototypenotyourselloutcause

massa and the big house is too good.
I am not your Aunt Jemima.

In my 8957 days of Black Womanhood I have learned this:
Be careful of what you say
of what you think
of what you do
because you never know who you're talking to.

TA-NEHISI COATES

Alice Flips the Script

You could never catch her
testifying at morning service,
shooting the shit at Quigleys,
or these other establishments
she will warn you of.

She is too Nubian for this.

She is that
recently crowned tofu queen,
emerging out of country-club culture,
where negroes toast '76 Chardonnay.
That Jack-and-Jill kid in rebellion,
head wrapped in all of Africa.
The Nordstroms connoisseur
turned student revolutionary.
She is the one her parents pray
you don't ask about.

College finds her as ultra-vegetarian,
cowrie-shelled-up,

kente-clothed-down,
and hair-dreaded like taxes.
She spends class time on the yard,
tapping the hidden power of estrogen,
bombing out the business school,
or flashing unread Fanon.

But she's Daddy's little girl.
She rolls up in a Lexus,
the one with the Ankh air-freshener
and the Sankofa rims to match.
Even the floor mats are mud cloth.

I peep her meditating under the flagpole,
like a Muslim praying under a crucifix.
She is not another bourgeoise honey-dip.
Sister is deep like sinkholes.
Hollow like them too.

A(E)RIN WILSON

Grenudita

i be zebrahead.
not too nappy   not too straight
fluff of "indian red"
luck of the irish in summer
rich Kenyan
you. can't. have. your. coffee.
        black.
in the winter
down to my waist

unbrushable   undeniably
    me.
where you get that weave?

    birth.
i slipped and fell
into a pool of genes fitting snug
around my tawny waist.
full pouty lips are mine too
talk about
thru my own average
flaps of skin.
the syllables rolling off my tongue
precisely   concisely
nicely   enticingly White.

girl, you def-nitly ain't frum da Ghetto.
go on back to yo mamma
'fore you get hert?

cursed to be blessed. de
                tested.
   in
     fested. my mind
un
  rested.

girl, you def-nitly ain't frum da Ghetto.

pseudosuburban   whiteuppermiddleclass
only black image they see smokin' crack
round the back
        in line at 9
           for that welfare check

shootin' and lootin'.   news
at 11 ... 10 ... 9 ... 8 ... 7 ... 6 ... 5 ... 4 ... 3 ...
and me.

but you're different. you're not really black.

thick nubian blood flows freely (through my veins).
     i am the same. with a twist.
¿es mexicana? ¿negra? ¿qué eres?
¡umm..yo s-toy a-mer-e-con-a!
     no no no ¿Qué Eres?
oohhh . . . yo soy ahhh ne-gra y blan-ca.
     ¡ah es mulatta, sí!
Mulatta?
     my entire existence narrowed down
to the identity of
       a mule.
an experiment.
       a mistake.
   sterile.
docile.
   a freak
     of nature. me.
          me?
             me!

miscegenation of the mind body and soul.
           soul. hit me
can'tsingcan'tdancecan'truncan't jump   much
betta than you.
     in time. about time. *stand*
fast old mule. stand fast. stand fast old mule.
   stand fast.

It's Hard!

It's hard being
    folded/licked
        creased
            at corners
                bluntly sharp
                black
              to hurt goin'
                in
                  and
                    out
It's hard
    being that
        dreaded Chicano
            African
                living with soul
                    split like my
                        people
        soul split
        like
Chicano⟵————————————⟶African
            it's
              hard
My sword is heavy
    cuz
      my spirit is
      light
Light parted down
    God's spine
        blood flooded
            between two middle
            riddles

free
    free
    FREESTYLIN'
my life
    braided intertwined
      in her
        Mayan feather
        firm shadow
bending prayer
    from
      black body
      to a fasting coyote
          singing to sunsets
sprinting
    with dusty
      Shaman
        chant pants
        from
        peace vexed
        cactus tomb stones
        it's hard!

Hard
  to take my
    yin and yang
    hand in hand
    y librar
      el huracán
        en mi corazón
          porque
      yo cannot swim across
        the noises
          in me cabeza
           that llamo me
nigga/
nigga/wetback
    halfbreed/nigga

What are you?

    nigga/wetback/halfbreedzebraniggawhatareyouniggahuhWHAT ARE
  YOU?

beener/zebra/nigga

WHAT ARE YOU?

             IT'S HARD Y'ALL

Hard

    to

    make art

        out of my

            double double

                talked talked

                    pains pains

            pulling pulling

                at at

            both both

                sides sides

        of of

            my my

                Chicano African

                Chicano African

  twice twice

      removed

  twice twice

      taught

          truth truth

            tossed tossed

        culture culture

           crossed crossed

              brain brain

                it's it's

                    HARD!!!

See

  my battle

  lies between the two

    to conjure up spirits

igualmente
　　　fruits
　　　　　y

　　　　　　　　mind
So I'm gonna beat my
　African drums
　　to my
　　　Aztec gods
　　　I'm going to be my Pharaoh
　　　　and taste my jazz
　　　　　live my reggae
　　　　　　y
　　　　　flamenco
　　　　　　y
　　　　　　　soca
　　　　　　　y
　　　　　　　　salsa
　　I will be that
　　　dreaded
　　　　　Chicano African
　　　cuz I am like my people
　　　　and my people are like me
　　　We　　　　　　We
　　　　are　　　　　are
　　　　　Chicano　　African
　We
　　are
　　　one
　　　　　AFRINO!!!
And we
　　are
　　　HARD!!!
We
　are
　　hard!!!

JOHN W. LOVE, JR.

Moment 9/The Woman

(From the One-Man Play Mocha Regions)

Yesterday, I was sitting in the corner of my glass bubble with my feet dangling over the edge watching you misunderstand me.

You thought I was the pin that dropped to the ground that made the sound but unfortunately nobody heard me because there was no silence around. And really if I were a straight pin, I was the straight pin in the haystack that everyone was looking for and because you didn't know where I was, you didn't know where to find me. Let's face it, I was much more specifically distinctive than you had ever imagined.

Now I see that you are lost. You're in a fog and did not understand or grasp the real meaning of anything that I was saying. Let me repeat myself.

Yesterday, I was sitting in the corner of my glass bubble with my feet dangling over the edge watching you misunderstand me.

Now you are thinking, ''. . . how can a glass bubble have a corner when we are making reference to a spherical entity, and how can one be inside a closed space and have anything dangling over any edge?'' Well I do have a corner and I do have an edge. Accept it.

My boyfriend just had a baby. He just gave birth to a gorgeous little girl. The pain of delivery nearly killed him but after the birth he had that euphoric glow that most new mothers have. I'm so happy for him. He was born pregnant and had been in labor for the past twenty-five years.

You see, this child is a spirit child. And already at five years old she shares his brain and his lungs. Sometimes she clouds his vision but mostly she has changed his focus.

Now, just two hours ago when she was thirteen, she aided him in understanding the frailties of my character and my justified paranoia about whether or not I'm pretty. And especially pretty to him. The three of us talked and laughed and drank decadently rich coffee. I went to the bathroom and by the time I got back she was already eighteen. She was so beautiful, so funny and incredibly wise for her age. Because she was inside her father, she helped him to understand how I felt when he hurt me. Pulled my hair. Slapped me in public. He was a new man. Not only was he in touch with his feminine side but he had a full-grown woman as his guide through the universe for the clearer understanding of all women. I felt so privileged to be at her birth and I told her so. I was the midwife, you know. During those last three years of his labor I made him breathe and push. I comforted. I cajoled. She was almost breech and her birth could have killed him, but I reached up inside and coaxed her to turn around the right way! It was a privilege for me to catch her, in my eager and loving arms, unwrap the strangling umbilical cord from around her neck, cut the cord, and lay her on her father's chest in order for her to recede into the recesses of his heart! I was the midwife and I was proud! . . .

That was my purpose in me and her father's relationship: to safely bring her into his life. The screaming, yelling, and thrashing that I took was all a part of his labor.

Now I guess I have some sort of perspective on that time he locked me out of the apartment in the dead of winter and I caught pneumonia. I guess that now I have some perspective on the many times he beat me unmercifully for looking too hard at other men! All that time he was in labor. He was having a baby.

About ten minutes ago, in the midst of my incredibly cathartic realizations, I dropped my coffee cup. Looked down. Looked up. And his eighteen-year-old girl was now twenty-five. Having dropped the coffee, I could suddenly wake up and smell it. I was displaced. She was a grown woman, an adult, and I was no longer needed. He had her and after all I had fulfilled my primary function: to help make this man a more whole human being by facilitating the realization—and expression!—of his feminine energy. Unfortunately, my beautiful bright twenty-five-year-old godchild had become an insufferable bitch. In a fit of rage I picked up a particularly long shard of the coffee cup, still steaming from its previous contents, and I shoved it where my goddaughter's heart was supposed to be. Surprisingly there was no resistance. And of course everything happened in slow motion. It was five minutes ago but already my memory is being distilled into snapshots. Coffee. Glass.

My hand. A fire up my spine and a numbness in my chest. The whir of the wind across my cool sweaty face as I twist violently from floor to chest. She screams. I killed her.

Unfortunately, I killed her father, too.

With spilled coffee, broken china, a turned-over chair, and two dead people on my kitchen floor along with the scattered snapshots of my memory . . . I called my therapist and told him that yesterday, I was sitting in the corner of my glass bubble with my feet dangling over the edge watching him misunderstand me and that perhaps it was a little too late and that therapy was out of the question. . . .

MARIAHADESSA ''EKERE'' TALLIE

Karma's Footsteps

We are the silent sex
whose screams
can't be heard in back alleys
or through paper-thin walls
we are mutes
whose heads can't be heard hitting walls
whose dignity can't be seen crawling on floors
forced to get on all fours
by husbands and boyfriends
who want things only we can give
    even when we have not made the offer
never thought to ask,
    wait
    or take NO for NO
since ''no'' has meant ''yes''
since the beginning of time
in womanspeak
a language translated by selfish men

who can't hear us
or see us
unless we're sucking their dicks
on movie screens
and even then
it's the sounds
of their own heavy breath
in our faces
which can't be seen
with their fingers scratching
pink, red, raw our throats
so we can't scream
so they can't hear
or be seen by ourselves
so we will walk the earth with secrets
and purses full of shame
and we will whisper our stories to walls and teddy bears
who will never tell us that subconsciously
we wanted to be ripped into fragments
and pushed beyond the sounds of "no"
echoing hollow
on someone else's lips
as I speak
as I am not heard
as someone else
won't be heard
or seen
or believed
tomorrow
we've had a million men march on our souls
while we cook the food
and mend the wounds
and hide the bruises
and whisper to walls
and watch our no's go up in smoke

and if I stay invisible
I'll start slittin' throats
so keep your eyes open
for things
you can't see
and listen out
for karma's footsteps

ABIODUN OYEWOLE

Future Shock

Can you Remember
or did you ever know
how beautiful you were
and the light was in your eyes
and your smile was for real
and we believed in each other
you cared for me
I cared for you
we were family
like trees in the valley
we grew straight and strong
and celebrated the blessing
of our lives in the Sun
Can you Remember
in some tiny corner
in the back of your mind
where death had not invaded
flowers grew
children laughed
without fear
of the bullets or the ballots

love nurtured us
like a Spring Rain
and Faith blossomed
in our hearts
Every day we'd wake up
Refreshed Reinspired Reborn
and we'd stay awake
even when we slept
Can you Remember
or has the middle passage
caused your memory lapse
made you forget your greatness
got you thinking
your life is sinking
like a slave ship
and you're going down
where you'll never be found
got you twisting and bending
and grinnin and sinnin
and never winnin for real
as you sit alone in the dark
embraced by an illusion
of the Blues
Can you Remember
it was a Spiritual thing
it was moving all through us
and we couldn't help but dance and sing
and sometimes
just jump up in the air
and fly away
it's in the music
we're coming back now
we're getting ready for tomorrow
steppin back from the hype
and refocusing our sight

on the 21st Century
this ain't no reentry
into slavery
it's time for some bravery
we never lost it
we always had it
no one can clock
how we really Rock
It's time for a Future Shock

chapter 5

Body &
Soul/
Celebrations

QUINCY TROUPE

Derrick Gilbert When I told several of my fellow poets that I was going to be interviewing you for this book, they all said, "D, you should interview Quincy for the Body & Soul chapter."

Quincy Troupe Really? Why they say that?

DG I don't know, but that's what I'd like to throw at you.

QT Well, I think that my work is within the whole body of African-American poetry. I think it's kind of eclectic, because of the influences that have impacted me. . . . Aimé Cesaire, Pablo Neruda, Langston Hughes . . . people like that who are kind of different . . . Amiri Baraka at one time, Allen Ginsberg . . . so my work is kind of eclectic and it's rhythmically based. I try to dance the language in a way that is rooted in music. Some people call me a jazz poet, but I don't think I'm a jazz poet—I might use jazz rhythms, but I also use blues and hip-hop rhythms . . . I use rock rhythms . . . I use anything that's at my fingertips. So I think maybe that's why people identify me with "Body & Soul."

Then I write about sports, and some very funny stuff. I also write poems that are revolutionary in the sense that they're trying to break the form. My poems deal with a lot of political matters, but they also deal with a lot of other things. And they deal with love and they deal with the spirit.

DG In your most recent book, *Avalanche,* you say: "A poet is supposed to either be dead or boring, or they have to be so pained that people can't find joy in it. That's not what I'm trying to do. I want to celebrate. I can be very sad, but I want to celebrate." Can you elaborate on this statement?

QT I want to celebrate life. You know, I think what happens with a lot of African-American people, and then African-American writers, is that we buy into what white people put on us. We buy into the pathos that we're these creatures who live in inner-city areas—that we're poor and that we have to write about all these depressing things. No! I believe in writing about those things, but I also believe in celebrating my life . . . and celebrating my spirit . . . and I believe in writing about joy, too.

I also believe in doing things rather than writing about it sometimes. You know, do something. That's my contribution. Stop drug dealers from selling stuff to these kids rather than talk about it. Make kids do their homework. Make these kids not jump on old people. We got to make these kids stop putting the graffiti on buildings. Protect our women—rather than talk or write about it. Do it. I'd rather do something rather than write about it. I believe in doing *it*— participating in the whole thing. I also believe in writing about it sometimes. But I also believe in letting my imagination fly. I mean, I think we are citizens of the world—I'm a citizen of the world. When I write, I'm not in competition with anybody—I'm writing mainly for myself . . . mainly for me. If somebody else likes it, *fine*. That's great. But I write for myself—for my own gratification. I want my imagination to flow.

DG What comes to mind when you think about the concept of "body and soul"?

QT When I think about "body & soul," I think about the soul. Freedom is about the soul. I believe in freedom, but I think that to be free you have to begin by believing that you are free. Nobody else can tell you that you are free. If a white person does something to me, I'm going to put instant justice on their ass. You know what I'm saying? I mean, if someone grabs my dreadlocks, I'm going to grab them upside their head. If a white woman comes up to me and grabs my dreadlocks and says, "Oh, I like your dreadlocks," I'm going to grab whatever hair she's got up there—and she won't do that again. In other words, I'm not going to say, "Don't grab me like that." I mean people take liberties with us because we don't stop them right away. Like last night I went to meet this Russian writer out here. Now, keep in mind, I got ten books . . . but this woman started to introduce me like "this is Quincy Troupe"—and instead of saying he's a fine writer, or author of so and so book, or he's a Professor at UC–San Diego—she says, "He's one of our kind of eclectic characters." I said, "Fuck you, I'm not an eclectic character—what are you talking about . . . don't introduce me to this man like that. You introduced him to me as a writer . . . so introduce me to him as a writer." Don't take that liberty because I'm an African-American, but that's what they do to us. They see you as this "other" or as this "beast." I don't care if you're Bill Cosby or Oprah Winfrey, they still see you as this other—but I refuse to let them deal with me like that; I want to deal as a human being in the world. And that doesn't mean I don't have concerns for people.

DG So what would you want to be the Quincy Troupe legacy?

QT I don't even think about it. I think that people should be remembered by their work and by their deeds. But I do want to be remembered as a person who worked hard to achieve some kind of place in literature. I mean I really worked hard for that. And I look at myself as a cultural worker—one who writes, one who puts on events, one who facilitates, one who edits, and all those sorts of things. So basically that's it—you know one who tried to extend the vocabulary, and one who tried to expand the limits of poetry and to smash barriers.

DG And what would be your advice to young writers?

QT I think that they should study. I think that they should study all the great writers of this century and of the last century. I think they should be aware of where they come from. I'm aware of where I come from at all times. I'm from St. Louis, Missouri: I come from the blues, I come from jazz, and I come from the church. I mean I grew up in the church, and I grew up around Black people—I know what I am and who I am . . . I know that. Never forget that. And so I think that people have to remember where they came from regardless of where they're at.

Writers also need to know where they want to go. And don't get tripped out by fame and money—it's just some momentary stuff. It's the spiritual we're after—the spiritual and freedom. It's the craft of writing. And we have to also understand that even though we are African Americans, we are going to have to get away from this hyphenated world. I don't know if that will happen soon, but that would be the ideal thing so that we don't become so balkanized in this country. I would like to see young people get away from balkanization in their writing—'cause I'm not interested in balkanization. I already know and believe that African Americans are beautiful . . . and ugly, too. I love that. I love that we are ugly and beautiful. And I know that I can be beautiful and ugly . . . and I know that I can be profound and stupid—I'm a human being, you see. Young writers have to be concerned with expressing themselves as human beings in the world. I already know that I'm an African American—as soon as I open my mouth . . . as soon as you see me with my wife . . . you see me with my kid—you know, I'm not trying to prove anything. But I am interested in contributing to humanity.

You see, if we are visionaries, what we have to do is to make people live up to what it is by setting examples of what it's supposed to be. It's not my problem if there's going to be Ku Klux Klansmens, or skinheads or whatever—that ain't my problem. It's really not—and there's nothing I can do about that. Now, if they come and put their hands on me now—I'm going to do something else to them; I'm going to talk another language then. You dig what I'm saying? If they try to harm my family or me, then that's something else—that's another deal. But we're dealing with the spiritual here. We're dealing with literature and craft and excellence. That's what I took from Langston Hughes, Melvin Tolson, Alain Locke, Zora Neale Hurston, and all those great writers who came before me.

So what I would say to young writers is this: They should study, read as much as they can, read writers from everywhere . . . and take whatever they need from them. And then write in the way that they feel comfortable. I feel comfortable the way I do things, the way I write—I really do.

DJ RENEGADE

Haiku

Jazz is
the way brown sugar
would sound
if it was sprinkled
in your ear

Duke Checks Out Ella As She Scats Like That

(To Quincy Troupe)

When Ella starts scatting
    she magnolia planted aside duke
playing that tonal Ouija board
and he swings her that slick, startled,
"woman you too bad" intonation,
    when the Duke do dat,
survival comes a god to marvel at,
even as the creator of Mt. Kilimanjaro
survival transmuted from sanctimonious
sanctioned genocide to African angels
swinging that singing like a trumpet made
of clouds and lightning, dropping walls
in a way that can only be called biblical,
metaphysical, in the umbilical between
heaven and Hades, where the devil
is an angel stringing sounds
    that defy atrocity.
When Ella starts scatting
and in an approaching layer of time
Nina Simone wails of Four Women,
after Lady Day cast southern trees
in a bright white light that not only
dreamily signaled death, but was death

197

and we are majestically resurrected
by Mahalia

    a miracle happens,
    continues to happen.
More than a mere resurrection,
a triumph over inhumanity.
When Ella starts scatting
'cause the trumpetmanArmstrong
momentarily forgot
his words
and spontaneously
started this ingenious tongue—
no mudafuck it ain't
    simply intuitive—
and James Brown
put horns, and strings, and funk,
and things
a primal electrified scream
all in the same thing,
thang, thing, thang, thang, thang.
And Papa's Got a Brand New Bag
makes us know it is never ending,
never ending, always something new
interpenetrating the old
like the digital ripping off
of the G-fada's analog riffs by the
hip-hopping Cab Calloways
of today,
a ghettoized tribute
to his funknosity
to global tenacity
to the Yoruba way
that lives in every beat

and b-note
created by our creators
when Ella scats
like that . . .

ART NIXON

Ju-Ju Man

(for John Coltrane)

How can you stand there &
how can you sit there &
be negative in your blackness????
When so manymany of your kind
your same black-kind died for your sins
mens who handled God's love & save you a piece &
blew you a God-kiss thru tarnished saxophones:
OUT OF THIS WORLD Trane stood
describing mean scenes in his Ju-Ju madness
possessed by God
possessed by God
Trane at the apex of priest MU/sicians
make'n wicked nigger-noise in the west
watch'm wicked critic white mens drop dead in '61
'cause he plays the Lord's Prayer backwards . . .
Make'n it happen anywhere: hot ivory offering
in the niteclub of the universe,
niggerlips sealed into the mouthpiece.
Hot ivory. Piano Smoke: BURN TRANE BURN!!!
BURN, BURN—Legba & Damballah & Ptah come

full circle out the bell of the baddest horn—
BURN TRANE, YEAH conjure up the spirits . . .
& Malcolm, who I thought wuz dead, stood bringing light &
Nat Turner sung a deafening love song—I saw Harriet!!—
felt her breathing in the stereo: TRANE TRANE TRANE

Coal TRANE hauling strange niggers into my living room
done conjured up the spirits
done conjured up the spirits
Unfamiliar faces of full-blooded Africans/long gone/
dancing in the music
dancing in the music
voices & visions escaping from the stereo/
nailing down the black-blue pain of AFRO BLUE nights.

Slack-jawed awe of flying negro saxophone-fingers
charred black by molten keys/his horn a glowing ingot
of supersonic tenor screams/chasing chord progressions/
all the way back to ancient African Kristallnachts:

Delicate hair-raised, chill-boned blues-scream
piercing of nights/village terror/civilized white
nite sticks & clubs waylay unsuspecting Africans
from the nite bush/pythons writhing/henna scream/
the sound of sub-Saharan skulls cracked/black feet scatter/
end run around kidnappers in dough-face/Africans stutter stepping
the pitch black/unfulfilled legacies broke down B-flat in
low moans/F-sharp pain of shackles/buckled down
African wrists
African ankles
African necks & knees . . .

Big boats slow rocking sagging deep in sea-green foam
Portuguese wood groaning the weight of black gold,
choice black booty of: gutbucket/zoot suit/razor slash/

sky hook/call & response/peanut butter & plasma/bebop & fertile
jelly roll/jesse owens & james brown/ali, smokey&baraka/
strange-looking fruit/& the talented tenth/8th 16th & 64th
notes as sheets of sound—git down git down TRANE:
blowing compassion & mercy, love & forgiveness on the horn's
upper register: KYRIE KYRIE KYRIE ELEISON
                    KYRIE KYRIE KYRIE ELEI—TRANE:

blowing PURSUANCE as El Haj Malik Shabazz! Azan! Allah-O-Akbar!
TRANE blowing jewels from the heart of the Lotus blossom:
                    AHM MANI PADME AUM
                    AHM MANI PADME AUM
                    AHM MANI PADME—TRANE:
blowing homage to the power beyond the beyond, and beyond the
great beyond, and beyond THAT beyond:
GATE, GATE PARA GATE, PARA SUM GATE, BODHISATTVA!
GATE, GATE PARA GATE, PARA SUM GATE, BODHI—TRANE:
blowing SUPREME enlightenment in the Latter Day of the Law:
                    NAM MYOHO RENGE KYO
                    NAM MYOHO RENGE KYO
                    NAM MYOHO RENGE KYO
                    NAM MYOHO RENGE—TRANE:
blowing past gadgets & me/chan/I/cal & tech/no/log/I/cal
im/a/ges of/the/world, past The Blues & funk, blowing &
screaming past perversion of self-hate & alienation, past
whatever white people call themselves AND me &
TRANE plays and

                    plays, and
                    we know   we are saved.

Milestones: September 28, 1991

The World is suddenly emptied of a certain
magical sound. A wotanic Silence invades our
consciousness like Romans invading Thebes.
A golden-master-trumpet no longer speaks.
Where is that intensity, that superb mystery,
that ultra-hipness, where has it flown?
We ask these brooding questions, lost in
the midnights of his wake: doomed to roam
this abyss minus a singular ray of light
from Ra's eye. One more innovative Master,
        priest-prophet, long gone!

Miles and miles of majesty, beauty, vision
romance; Classicism born in an Afrikan mode . . .
And nightly, a lovely sepia diva bitterly weeps;
for he is beyond the fame and devastation, pain
and desolation, profane revelations that America
offers Black men. His wounds have bled enough!
His falcon soul has flown beyond thunders
of the rising sun. A man, a vision, a life
brilliantly conceived and achieved—like a pharaoh
grandly shaping his age, royally, Suddenly,
this Dark Lord stumbles, falls, and the World
trembles . . . Westwards, in the bleak dusk and chill
Silence of a "square" hospital, he sighs, begins
        his Final Solo—and we weep!

I Remember 1983

i remember 1983
as the year we got our drums back,
the year you could find black boys
gliding down the halls instead of walking,
the same year preppie black girls,
attending their first ghetto school,
learned to dance the prep' like everybody else.
we carried contraband:
25¢ now and later packs
bought from the corner store,
smuggled into the public school system,
and thought we were doing something
when we ate them in reading lab, undetected.
but none of that really ever
challenged the status quo.
what had to be stopped
was the knocking.
monday morning homeroom
brought the noise:
fresh new beats, mastered over the weekend.
teachers made their rounds threatening detention,
but once the call was sent,
the response was bound to follow.
and for the rest of the week
you would hear knocking and beat boxing
echoing through the halls.
black boys and black girls
who had never learned
that drums had been outlawed
cause a beat could be dangerous

had rhythms in our heads,
and they had to come out.
and it didn't matter when,
or where,
or how loud.
yeah, i remember 1983:
when hip-hop was called rap,
and people had names like Turbo,
and parachute pants were so cool
you could wear the same pair twice in a week
and still be fresh . . .
but what's funny
is that the only thing that still matter
is the beat.
cause it rocks
on and
on and
on and on . . .
we let it flow
and it don't stop!

DEFARI HERUT

Gems

Rhymes are gems I run tracks like Ben Johnson/Dick Vitale said my style was
awesome—
P.T.P. M.C. prime time precisely word to brothas I gets Isley—
And voyage to Atlantis Black sea world of panthers where brothas don't
question they answer—
Mathematically with lyrics of strategy the goal is to remedy this world of the
wack m.c.—

Exactly!—Defari lyrical athlete find me in the final heat of the Olympic track
meet for m.c.'s—
This kid he's not the average I'm on the rise son as if my name was Back-
stage Laminate—
I got a cabinet of members all who possess spectacular vernacular blazin'
thru contenders—
I remember when Hip Hop was genuine when gimmicks were limited m.c.'s
were magnificent
shows were omnipotent the crowd was all feelin' it if a kid had skill on stage
yo he'd reveal it—
But nowadays mad m.c.'s need lessons in stage presence instead of claimin'
they represent—
While I enterprise maintain stay awake and wise what you hear is what you
get no Lies no Disguise!

Rhymes are Gems.

MARLON C. WILLIAMS (POETX)

Blood, Sweat, and Fears

Red, clear,
No color for fear
Cheers fill my ears
As I impress my peers
Athletes appear to do well and steer
Up and down fields while changing their gears
Gauze and bandaged become uniform wear
Casts for breaks, stitches for tears
Carried off to applause as everyone stares
Temporarily damaged or confined to a wheelchair
Blood's in the air,
For those who dare,

To sweat all year and fight past their fear
Of the media's jeers
And opponents' swears
Tempers flare as the kickoff nears
I surely and truly hope the Lord hears
My prayers to escape the Blood, Sweat, and Fears.

T'KALLA

Nuns in the Basement of God

In the basement of the opera house
there are
nuns
who break-dance
on laid-out cardboard
        in search

with fingertips that dream of
ghetto cornrows
as
their practice

behind closed doors
their muse is hip-hop

with visions of concrete moons
they paint pictures of
their patron saint

melle mell
over flashes grand-mastered of a furious
five

but their love of the break beat
has been lacerated by the god
they work for

in this hall of hollow
music
they dream of running
their fingers through the
head of
man

to the track
they spin
drinking whiskey from wineglasses
while wishing that
the convent had a
time
clock

so they could end their day and be free
for a
                minute
ride the A train and
   kick
ballistics with soul

but instead they
wipe sweat from their
brow with black cloth in preparation
for one
last spin on cardboard

in the basement of the
opera house they close
their eyes and kiss

their music from its
hips to its mouth

CHEZIA THOMPSON-CAGER

Praise Song for Katherine Dunham: A Choreopoem

feet unbound
walk the Earth
In padded souls
stretched into flexing
as conversation

dancez?

Feet whispering mysteries
in solaced grace

tempering drum calls
from the Earth herself
a language where
movement becomes literature
and art ceases to be static
even in the Western Tradition

dancez?

feet as articulate transformers
of nuance and gestures

a measurement of the tonal quality
languishing in space warped
theories of cultural exchange

dancez?

You swim Du Bois' Dark Water
and find Marie LaVeau's Congo Square
join Paule Marshall's Ring Dance
only to ascend to Wole Soyinka's Fourth Level
effortlessly
where you command the drum and the rattle
to declare our names—our birthright

dancez?

We are river maidens
whose beauty as motion and dream
ride atop Josephine Baker's
cakewalk blues in East St. Louis
The Maroon's powerful Kumina
in Jamaica
Elegant Quadrilles in New Orleans' Ballrooms
or a wild Charleston in Harlem's Savoy

where acting out the drama of NOMMO
the drama of one woman's celestial discourse
with the elements changed
the world forever

The Dance is
for healing
The Dance is
for communicating

The Dance is
for Transforming Time
The Dance is
for recreating a passage
between worlds
The Dance invites
the Living and the Dead
to the same feast
on the Axis
where you sit Madrina
watching us
chant your promise
that if we believe
we can traverse the air in motion
we can ride space
speaking in the tongues of angels

CANDICE M. JENKINS

Poem for Tracy (Chapman)

it was my mother who loved you first—
she who listens to music so infrequently that it
sounds against her ears as shocking and rich as
the world to a newborn's eyes—and i knew you as
simply a warmth of hair, skin, gleaming from
an album cover bronze and silent i was
a child, tracy

i am a woman now, and you are rich and
shocking to my ears, you are a splash, cool liquid pouring,
you are an unfolding, a birth, you are like the blue-warm
oil of dawn, a voice scented and sweet, and dark as life, tracy

would you sing a song for me and all the times i've
needed blackwomen standing
beside, before, beneath,
above me, promising, breath as gentle and hollow as
moonlight? tracy

would you turn and see me, would you
sing me a dream, would you sing and sing and
convince this world we can
begin again
begin with our eyes lifted like banners
of love, flying in the wind, begin
today, tracy

i think your face is
as solid as a length of
silver stone, weighing in my hands,
i want to greet you in a voice that rises
clear and ringing, as smooth as waxy skin on
leaves, tracy
i want you to understand
what is at work here, your song
is sleek and strong as sealskin

and you
tracy
are as grained as
polished wood, as still and
as lovely, woman

you are a magicmaker
        woman

Flying High

(For Gil-Scott Heron)

Bubble, clearheaded man
with Third Eye, searching—
haunting your own self

with a mind full of razors
flying high

Sage of our ragged years,
your tongue pushing cells on fire
thrusting ash aside
to unveil streaked faces

your mind on razors
flying high

Your words,
like chipped stones turned daggers,
call themselves hedging
fenced souls

your mind on razors
flying high
And we echo back to you:

Go on 'head with it, Gil—
pass the bowl, brother
fill our ancient ruins with
your piped music. Together,

let's bandage revolution
and its—Aries
over still-watered cravings

our minds full of razors
flying high

KAREN WILLIAMS

Kissing Keys

(For Ashford and Simpson & Winbush and Isley)

Tell me, is it hard to wrap your tongue and fingers around a note
until it oozes honey, marrow, blood, a plaintive to joyous wail,
a moonlit serenade that wings our blazing hemispheres,
roosts in hearts ruby-throated birds singing
in time twisted Baobabs in the African distance
to the thrum of natives pulsating under a rust colored sun

and is it hard to interpret nights of hot chocolate breathing,
trailing lips, nails and tongues, digging deep into backs,
excavating bottomless forbidden grooves, bottomless forbidden
groves and loving it as fragrant sweat pools, drips, hisses,
cooling the fire spreading from my pressed to your chest breasts to
the floor of my grander than grand canyon

and it is hard to define how good a fresh olive tastes chilled,
pimento carefully removed then placed strategically on the tongue
and pushed onto yours with a full-mouthed kiss
stained with your almond scent

and is it hard to simulate on heat-sensitive paper,
the extemporaneous give and take, the is it real good to ya

push and pull, the wanton thrusts, absorption of hot and sticky,
a tender love born a mile high, fondled deep in blue pool waters,
on lazy afternoons when the children are taking their naps
and it just feels good to rock, roll, to do a slow grind
in the middle of the living room floor then recline on the sofa,
naked under a soft throw to listen to Billie's "Don't Explain" with
a cold sip of wine after a tasty requited shower because
things like this we used to do before the spare tire followed
the baby

and is it hard kissing keys, telling the ebony and ivory I Love You
in ways we will hunt to feel it, in ways pitch and tone will
understand in soft, hard, hard, soft, pianoforte strokes
to later be heard the world over in adagios, melodies, ballads,
lyrics ever so fondly remembered because you laid your joy, your
troubles down on wax, have loosed your love, your life
into my song, have translated your respect, the power of love
and love of each other, of man and woman, lovemaking and humankind
into a rhythm, passion and blues until you some of us
have never known or are we just free, fiery, attentive lovers,
already floating on our own natural high?

PATRICIA SMITH

Asking for a Heart Attack

(For Aretha Franklin)

Aretha. Deep butter dipt, burnt pot liquor, twisted sugarcane,
Vaselined knock knees clacking extraordinary gospel,
hustling toward the promised land in 4/4 time, Aretha.
Greased and glowing awash in limelight, sanctified moan
'neath spotlight, turning ample ass toward midnight,

she the it's-all-good goddess of warm corn bread
and bumped buttermilk, know Jesus by His *first* name,
carried his gospel low and democratic in rollicking brownhips,
sang His drooping corpse down from that ragged wooded T,
dressed Him up in something shiny, conked that Holy head of hair,
then Aretha rustled up bus fare and took the Deity downtown.
They coaxed the DJ and slid electric until the lights slammed on,
she taught Him dirty nicknames for His father's handiwork.
She was young then, thin and aching, her heartbox shut tight.
So Jesus blessed her, He opened her throat and taught her
to wail that way she do, she do wail that way don't she
do that wail the way she do wail that way, don't she?
Now every time 'Retha unreel that screech, sang Delta
cut through hurting to glimpse been-done-wrong bone,
a born-again brother called the Holy Ghost creeps through that.
And that, for all you still lookin', is religion.

Dare you question her several shoulders, the soft stairsteps
of flesh leading to her shaking chins, the steel bones
of a corseted frock eating into bubbling sides,
zipper track etched into skin,
all those faint scars,
those lovesore battle wounds?
Ain't your mama never told you
how black women collect the world,
build other bodies onto their own?
No earthly man knows the solution to our hips,
asses urgent as sirens,
titties familiar as everybody's mama,
crisscrossed with pulled roads of blood.
Ask us why we pray with our dancin' shoes on, why we
grow fat away from everyone and toward each other.

Collage

inside its own mystery, the poetic line circles back & forth
moving between & around parameters, shifting questions
like chess moves, words strike at the heart of syntax
everywhere, deploy their chord changes as notes in musical phrases
or cluster like drones silhouetted in a honeycomb if the voice box breaks
& its tone is always dry as bone, its volume mannered, meticulous,
never raised above a humming whisper—but is a thin straight line
cutting through the graph of an EKG heart-monitoring machine
doodad—no accents there, no nuance, no effervescence
as in a spew bursting spumescent from a sudsing waterfall—

the petals of spray holding faces in that foaming articulation there—
when dashed over stones, in swelling deep basin bottoms, fingerlike
plumes dancing upward, when the water hits the surface hard & is bridged
across the light to a shimmering point by a miracle of arching rainbows

where the sun rides up through the transparency of misting flesh
& the veiling water's cloudlike breath is atomized in flicks
shadow catchers pick & catch in black & white or luminous
color frames, shot through their optic lenses, like nirvana
& can be a luminous moment of pure magic when snatched
from a thrilling once-in-a-lifetime moment & is crystallized there

inside an image of what air jordan used to create, when he soared high
above the rest, up there in space, as if he were jimi hendrix, or the prince
of darkness, miles dewey davis playing blue on *aura*—all playing mantras
deep inside themselves, without a clue of bullshit or hesitation,
without fear of switching gears, as they soloed to bloom into flowers
of their syncopated magic, shining, high up above imitations—
their imaginations flying somewhere perhaps out over the dome of montana
where the eyes see clouds as shows, or bruising battleships

216

cruising wide open currents of wind, light, skies blue as eyeballs there
of some scandinavian mountain climber bird-tracking through snow
upward, toward some summit, where we fix now our arrowing gaze
& where a flock of birds is a burst of syllables—as in a sprinkling of black
notes as winged chords—scattering themselves across our view
as if they were a crew of dark dots tacked to the surface of some painting—
a collage of impressions flung there as if they were a herd of nervous eyes
hyperventilating, as in the body language of new-age hiphop cultural stew,
the colors there dazzling, the aroma of their digable planet mack attacks
sizzling staccatic, pungent inside blooming spices of words flung everywhere
as clues of generational breakdown—what else can eye tell you
except the world is square instead of round, that there's no meaning

to the silly question of if one walks a straight line or staggers up a hill
but an argument over shape, you know, apples or oranges, skinny or fat,
or the reason some blockheaded gringos slosh beer & act out roles of ugly
americans in mexico, deep inside the microwave oven of their fogs—perhaps
ratcheting up an urge of jeffrey dahmer, a bar or two of nuclear burnout
blues—whacked-out on the bullshit tip of walt disney's mouseketeering trip
& stretched out on sun-fried sands of cash-&-carry brains, oozing madly

all over gridlocked freeways of L.A., every day, hey, we're talking about
   MTV
informational meltdown here, a blizzard of cardboard images hacked up
& dropped in a frenzied celebration of confetti on a ticker-tape parade—

eye mean, the whole whirl changed after that mushroom cloud bloomed
& left all those incinerated shadows inked into the world's collective brain
but whose children then rose up through schematas of grids & computer
chips to strangle the money flow in the throats of the mad bombers
of the west & diverted away a gaggle of greenbacks to their squirrels nests
located somewhere in official tokyo—imitations of cowboys & rockers there
too, at best a weird fascination with the culture of those who bombed them—
somewhere in the west, on a clear day in June, when eyes seem to see
forever, reaching out, covering space from perception to recognition, what is
seen, though, might not always be true, but is only possibility, suggesting

217

what *might* be true, as in a mirage when our eyes tell us what we see
there, square dancing in front of us, are xeroxed copies of middle-american
porkers, who are copies of other copies of other copies & on & on & on
ad infinitum, though what might be truer is that those copies we think
we see are only white styrofoam sculptures of george segal, unctuous
illusions caught up in shifting light outlining magical tricks the art of seeing
plays on our terrified minds—images grafted there through our eyes
wheedling spin doctors of influence lay down on us—as in a photo of air
jordan, seemingly walking up there, through space, his outstretched arm
& hand holding a basketball, his leonine body a picture of lean beauty

strength & grace & the black & white colors showing no tensions at all

chapter 6

Catch the Fire

SONIA SANCHEZ

Derrick Gilbert What inspired you to write your poem "Catch the Fire"?

Sonia Sanchez I was talking to brother Bill Cosby on the telephone about going up to New York to do something. And we started this conversation about our children—about what they're doing and where they're moving to. Somehow he asked me to write a poem to our children about what they should be doing, and I actually wrote the poem overnight. Now, the title came about because Bill said to me: "Where's the fire?" And when I started writing the poem, I kept hearing in my head: "catch the fire," "catch the fire," "catch the fire"— the fire that we've all had as a people.

Tony Medina What was the poetic climate like in the sixties and seventies? And how do you see the poetic climate today?

SS When we first came, I think we had to create an audience for the type of poetry we had decided we were going to do. It was not that I hadn't written poetry before, because I had published in such places as *The Minnesota Review, The Transatlantic Review, The New England Review*—making my name through that slow publishing route. But in the midst of all this, Malcolm came on the scene. And prior to Malcolm, the poems I had written did not necessarily indicate that I was Black in any active fashion— to say it nicely; the poetry had politics, but we just didn't identify who we were or what we were about. So, with the advent of Malcolm, a lot of that poetry that we were writing—at least that I was writing—made a complete turn and began to identify oneself as a Black woman. We began to write about what it was to see Black soldiers in Vietnam disproportionately represented. Several interesting political questions like that began to surface. But the main thing was the idea of someone saying you were Black—and that was beautiful, and that was good, and that was okay, and that was political, and that was interesting. Then there was the possibility that you were the first human being on the planet earth, and that you had a history. So what Malcolm did was that he made us all go into the libraries; in a sense, he began our research. You see Malcolm caused—and most scholars miss this point with him—Malcolm caused an eruption, and a disruption, and an evolution, and a revolution. He caused us to open our eyes and see things in a new way. Malcolm was our teacher, and we were in school always when we were around him listening to him talk. So Malcolm changed the poetic climate; he made us start writing about these things.

DG And what was the "vibe" during this period—a period that is labeled the Black Arts movement?

SS I don't think you can simplify it. I mean, there were a lot of folks writing who weren't part of the Black Arts movement. What was significant about the Black Arts movement in Harlem was that [Amiri] Baraka and Larry Neal brought together a different group of people— musicians, painters, dramatists, dancers, and writers of all sorts. After that ended in New York, we all sort of migrated to California and started Black Studies. Therefore, it was transplanted, in a sense, from the East Coast to the West Coast. It was in California where we met such people as Ed Bullins and Marvin X; we learned about the Black Arts movement West. But the important thing about us is that . . . although we were writing politically oriented poetry, and although we were organized, we never excluded other people. If you had something to read, "Go on . . . you can read it." We had a generosity of spirit. You didn't have to be like us to be included; all we wanted you to do was get up there and be good poets.

TM How do you see the poetry scene today?

DG And along with that, what advice would you give today's young poets?

SS I hope that all of you who take poetry seriously will learn not to be competitive. I hope that if you choose to participate in poetry slams, that you bring some kind of humanity to it. You see, we should not be on some auction block somewhere selling our poetry in that fashion. And I have to say that right now I'm against the whole idea of slams; I don't think we need them. The second part about that is that I think it's important to learn the craft of poetry; I've always said that. By that I mean we must always be in the process of becoming good craftspersons. For example, I consider myself always a student of my craft—which means I am always willing to learn and that I'm always willing to listen. So if you go back and check out everything that I've written, you will see that I have always dealt with form. Now, the point with form, that we have to understand, is that form doesn't reform you or malform you; and as an African American, and as an African, you can take anything and do with it what you want to do. So when young writers come up to me and say that they want to do a book, I always tell them to learn the craft more. I mean one day you might have that book out and not even like the idea that that book is out there.

We have to learn that it's not about a book—it's about understanding how connected we are to our tradition of great writing. We are connected to a tradition of good writing; we are connected to a tradition of writing that people came through learning on their own. But the point is that if you have people who can help you and have your interest at heart, then it's important that you read as much poetry as you can . . . and everything that you can. It's very, very important that you study poetry and understand that it's a cruel master, because it will whip your ass sometimes—but you will look up and say "thank you" and come on back into the wind and begin that process again. Poetry, to me, is the greatest genre on the planet earth because it is an exacting mistress and master—because it does kick your ass; but it also sings to you sometimes in the morning. When you do a poem, and you say it and go out on the porch and say it again, and it sings to you, you have to thank the Creator for making you a poet. And I know that that's what the first African poet felt—that's what she felt and that's what he felt . . . and that's what we all should feel. It is not about commercialism out there—it's about saying simply *"I am a poet!"* That alone brings with it a history and a herstory. *"I am a poet!"* That brings with it excellence and courage. *"I am a poet!"* That brings with it my beauty and the beauty of the genre. *"I am a poet!"* That brings with it the beauty of the act and the beauty of the song. *"I AM A POET!"*

SONIA SANCHEZ

Catch the Fire

(For Bill Cosby)

(Sometimes I Wonder:

What to say to you now
in the soft afternoon air as you
hold us all in a single death?)

I say—

Where is your fire?

I say—

Where is your fire?

You got to find it and pass it on
You got to find it and pass it on
from you to me from me to her from her
to him from the son to the father from the
brother to the sister from the daughter to
the mother from the mother to child.

Where is your fire? I say where is your fire?
Can't you smell it coming out of our past?
The fire of living. . . . . . Not dying
The fire of loving. . . . . Not killing
The fire of Blackness. . . Not gangster shadows.

Where is our beautiful fire that gave light
to the world?

The fire of pyramids;
The fire that burned through the holes of
slaveships and made us breathe;
The fire that made guts into chitterlings;
The fire that took rhythms and made jazz;
The fire of sit-ins and marches that made
us jump boundaries and barriers;
The fire that took street talk and sounds
and made righteous imhotep raps.
Where is your fire, the torch of life
full of Nzinga and Nat Turner and Garvey
and Du Bois and Fanni Lou Hamer and
  Martin and Malcolm and Mandela.

Sister/Sistah. Brother/Brotha. Come/Come.

CATCH YOUR FIRE. . . . . . .DON'T KILL
HOLD YOUR FIRE. . . . . . . .DON'T KILL
LEARN YOUR FIRE. . . . . .DON'T KILL
BE THE FIRE. . . . . .DON'T KILL

Catch the fire and burn with eyes
that see our souls:
     WALKING.
     SINGING.
     BUILDING.
     LAUGHING.
     LEARNING.
     LOVING.
     TEACHING.
     BEING.

Hey. Brother/Brotha. Sister/Sistah.
Here is my hand.
Catch the fire . . . and live.

live.

live.

livelivelivelive.

livelivelivelive.

live.

live.

KALAMU YA SALAAM

Soon One Morning, I'll Fly Away

Where does heart rest, breath originate
where is buried afterbirth, what world is flavored
with the sweetness of mother milk, spiced by a jigger
of father essence unmercifully purifying, trellised
by the communal touch of kind and kin heat tough
as the sun spear of cloudless August noon

While we tread life's tribulation bridge and seek to craft
some small sweet space from the loam of this bitter earth
whether in shit storm or sun shade there is but one certain
fuel to animate our keeping on, and that be our deep
belief tear-crystal, regardless of which exploiter
we labor beneath, the end of our existence is that we black
Weary travelers, being not from here, must death rise & return
to the spirit space wherein we dwelled before we were birthed

JERRY W. WARD, JR.

At the Border of Constant Disaster

only the infants
too young to know of tribes
can travel to the bottom
and give outrage a name

and answer through sleep
a permanent defiance

only the infants
too pure to know false tenderness
can make the stiff comfort of cardboard
softer than the lava of exile

and anchor through sleep
a permanent defiance

only the infants
too wise to contend with truth
refuse the bread of death and pestilence
refuse the wine of war and famine

and assume through sleep
a permanent defiance

Doris

"Slavery is a living wound under a patchwork of scars."
　　　　　—Kwadwo Opoku-Agyemang

She draped naked buildings with daydreams,
stepped over shattered glass that once
held liquor and flashing fantasy,
painted whole families on boarded windows,
a portrait of mama, papa, cousins and grands,
renamed the made-up children, gave them
spirituals and kenté filling the puzzle with song.

"Weren't we captives not submitting slaves?
Weren't we captives not submitting slaves?
Remember we resisted, we resisted."

She still saw the wounds from the Passage,
when Dahomey, Ebo and Asanti were stuffed
in the bowels of boats and the spines of grown
men and women were chained to curve like embryos,
light blocked from eyes, tongues struck silent,
so many days in darkness, we forgot our names.

"I keep a picture of the sun
tucked in the corner of my mind.
I said, I keep a picture of the sun,
the way it rises at home,
tucked in the corner of my mind.
When they tell me, I must be born again,
I say, I never died."

Miracle

Headline:
Another Church Is Burned!
Triple K Membership Increased Threefold!
Anti-Jewish/Anti-Muslim/Anti-Immigrant/Anti-Everybody Sentiments on the
  Rise!
Another King Is Beaten!
Another X is marked!
Another Riot Has Occurred!

But
Stop the stress
Or . . . what do they say
Stop the presses

Let's turn off the 5 o'clock/6 o'clock/7 o'clock bad news
Let's shred the no-good news newspapers
Let's gag/mute/and shut up the talk/talk/talk
(What are you talkin' about?)
Talk shows
Let's stop the stress and the press
And tune into the twenty-four-hour miracle network

And
At the top of our news . . .
A rainbow has been reported on the playground
That's right
There's a rainbow of children
Runnin'/swingin'/jumpin'/climbin'/and just havin' fun together
And the only race they know
Requires them to run

And to run fast (Tag, you're it!)
And there's harmony flowin' in their games
And it's a beautiful thing
And it's a miracle
It's a miracle

And
Our sources have revealed that
Two people have just climbed in love
He's lavender, she's turquoise
She's maroon, he's teal
He has polka dots, she has stripes
Or she's blue and he's blue too
Or he's a he
And she's a she
And it's all cool
'Cause they're in love
Not in fever
Not in fashion
Two just in love
And your eyes may frown
But
Hey
LOVE HAPPENS!
And
When it does
It's a miracle
It's a miracle

And
This just in
Two old men meet on a young park bench

And feed pigeons
And watch kids play
But mostly they share each other's memories
And it doesn't really matter that
One man's Black and that the other's white
Or that thirty years earlier
The Black man couldn't even pick up trash in this park
But what matters is
There's pigeons to feed
And kids to watch
And what matters is
They're friends
And it's a miracle
It's a miracle

And
We interrupt this poem to let you know
That you are exquisite
That you are a rainbow
That Love Happens
And that life is
Quite magically a
Waterfall of miracles

Our Spirit Stands

Tears of disillusion have always fallen from our black eyes.
Our Ancestors have always carried burdens like boulders,
raised children in the strange light
of crosses burning in their yards.

Our tired trek has not always been written in books,
but we sing, dance and write poems
on how we have proceeded one heavy step after another.
Now, the first place of our solace, the place where we shout joy
is coming down.

Churches raining tear stained ashes around our weary feet
Hope dreaded, twisted and gnarled
like arthritic fingers
Yet, Our Spirit Stands.

Puffed up like deep purple mountains
raised high like brown holy hands,
cried out like a chorus of soulful hallelujahs,
Our Spirit Stands.

We whisper heated prayers of protection.
Seek to be cradled like whispered hymns
in the arms of God.

We meditate on an end to this madness.
Focus on the good.
Cower not to the shriveling acts of the demented,
rise above these white hot crimes.
We kneel not to this hatred, bend not to these evil deeds.

233

We stand steadfast in the midst of these fires.
It will not burn the crucifix in our eyes.

We will not dash our hope among the jagged rocks of injustice
but step on mounds as old as time.
Pilgrim till what is lost is found.
We will caress the stranger within us.
Find hope in each other's trembling eyes.
We will rise above this burning chaos,
mount up on the wings of eagles
and let faith fly like doves from our hands.
When the dust of these disasters settles, in a cry of faith
We will resound.
        Our Spirit Stands
           Our Spirit Stands.

JABARI ASIM

Mumble the Magic Words

Come, claim your wings.
Lift your life above the earth,
return to the land of your father's birth.

Come, unbend your back.
Let us fade together in a trick of light.
Let us gather stars and ride the night,
never forgetting those who've forgotten
beneath the lash and sting of cotton.

kum kunka yali,
kum . . . tambe!
buba yali
buba tambe

Mumble the magic words.
Seize the sky as soaring birds.

Just Us

Black poems will
feed Black minds but
who will put chakula
into the children's bellies
and make them full with nourishment

Black poems will
cleanse Black souls but
who will give proper attention
to sisters hungry for time
and respect

Black poems will
love thin sheets of white paper but
who will develop proud black you
who will nurture thick black hearts
who will create strong black families

It must be us . . .
Just Us!

Eye & Eye

eye & eye
     am free of not you
          but thee
               sings through me
                    this is
                         that he is
                             something there/

eye & eye wait
     for the Where
          & the When
               twixt the birth
                    & doom of the is
                         that will always be
                             in earnest the difference/

eye & eye
     of the How
          Who we are
               the now, my friend
                    that becomes the then
                       that once was
                             the stardust of skies/

eye & eye rise
     to the plainest of things
          the simple question
          the germ of the is
               supreme constellation of thee & me
                    this cosmic water
                       the Why of the just/

eye & eye sleep
    the idea of love
        incarnate the feeling
    the dream that drinks
        the serene essence that quenches
           the thirst of this trust
              grows the goodness in us/

SAUL WILLIAMS

Recitation

i could recite the grass on a hill
and memorize the moon

i know the cloud forms of love by heart
and have brought tears to the eye of a storm

my memory banks vault of autumn forests
and amazon riverbanks

and i've screamed them into sunsets
that echoed in earthquakes

shadows have been my spotlight
as i monologue the night
and dialogue with days
soliloquies of wind and breeze
applauded by sun rays

***

we put language in zoos
to observe caged thought
and tossed peanuts and p-funk at intellect

and mothafuckas think these are metaphors
i speak what i see
all words and worlds are metaphors of me

my life is authored by the moon
footprints written in soil

(i am)
the fountain pen of martian men
novelling human toil
and, yes, the soil speaks highly of me
when earth-seeds root me
poet-tree

and we forest forever with recitation

SONJA MARIE

Dream Fix

I'm a Dreamer in Ready Stance
Shaking and Sweating into a Crack Dance
Show How Anxious My Soul Is
Fill the Pipe Up with Motivation Kid
Pass it Pronto—Don't Expect for Me to Let Go
Cuz It's My Turn
Causing Instant Earthquakes to Rumble
While My Existence Tumbles

I'll Die to See My Success Burn
Making Puffs of Smoke So My Family in Yonkers
Can Feel the High
Put on My Old School Skates with the Stopper
Now I'm Ready to Glide
Scratching Deep into My Armpits
Digging Hard for Strength So I Can Smell It
Holding Tightly to His Power
Workin' to Let Go
Like He Was a Snickers Bar
Thirsting for Answers
Fire in My Throat
Like Ned to the Liquor Store
I'm Pheenin'
I'm Dreamin'
I'm Doin'
I'm Groovin'
I'm Searchin'
And Lovin'
Here and Now in the Mix
I'm a Crack Head in Ready Stance
For My Dream Fix . . .

I'm a Crack Head for My Dreams

Sister Roll

Look at them fly
these wild Sankofa birds
Middle Passage Divas
workin' the spot for points

Cross
stage and desert
they roll
like Grandma's bread pins
over heart
they current
a bevy of daughters, sisters, elders

They come
in Kente speaking mud cloth
arms like jembes
they slap evil spirits down
feet stomp
some move with Motherland precision
others do the cabbage patch
with the same love from above

'Taint no Wodabi here
these sisters know where they're goin'

They wade
they wade like Harriet
deep and in water
sweatin' the crossing
telling no tales dead

Just move

You wild Negritudes
y'all don't need to be blessed
sweat
dripped from the palms of Oshun
shine your head
like pomades from above

Let lord come down
cause somebody gone get over tonight

The drums come
entering souls
callin' names
ain't no bitch or hoes
up in here
this stage is holy.

YONA HARVEY

Sonia Told the Women

wise
as west coast waters
and seashells
singing
melodies
to spirits of the seas

you are bold
as new york city

arms
spread wider
than texas
closing hugs
hot as houston sun

sweeter than
washington apples
the brown sugar
of florida sand

as funky as
cincinnati sunshine
content as earth
between georgia toes

deeper than
the canyon
cool as
colorado snow

walk your beauty
all over this land

The Fire in the Drum

(For Matt Crawford: 1903–1996)

How do we embrace a blazing revolutionary spirit
How do we hug and massage a bay burning legacy
How do we booby-trap a courageous fire
And suspend its essence on root-strong fingertips
And flick calcium-enriched flames to burn free
The manifold hapless frozen souls
Who carelessly make the world a silly/chilly
Frosty the snowflake place
How do we resist the deceptively warm temptations of complacency
And butterfly-stroke our way upstream
In subzero/subhuman oil-burdened waters
Even when our thighs/forearms/and bottom lips
Are memory-shackled and identity-gagged
With 400-year-strong
Transatlantic seaweed
How do we ice-pick through the pain
How do we chisel through the chills
How do we defrost the frozen lives
How do we resist/rebel/and Re-Heal
Let us begin by calling out the names of those
Who gracefully held their breath in smoke-burdened crevices
So that future generations could effortlessly breathe
We mouth-to-mouth names like
Sojourner/and Denmark/and Gabriel/and Harriet/and Walker
And Dunbar/and McCoy/and Nat
We ignite flames with high-octane names like
Fannie Lou/and Mary Church/and Carter G/and Ida B/and A. Philip
And Ossie D/and Ruby Dee/and Marcus G/and Jimmy B/and W.E.B.
We conjure wildfires/wildflowers/and wildlife with names like

Louise/and Rosa/and Patterson/and Bethune/and Drew/
And Medgar/and Ella/and Angela/and Mahalia/and Martin/
And Marvin/and Aretha/and Ali/and X
We invite the sun's passion to sizzle flesh by shouting names like
Trane/and Sonia/and Gwendolyn/and Dizzy/and Micheaux/and Roach/
  and Dunham/and
Catlett/and Barnes/and Lawrence/and Bearden/and Morrison/and Ringgold/
  and Mfume
And Maxine/and Dellums
And if these names don't snap/pop/and crackle with familiarity
We parachute into the belly of volcanoes
And formally introduce ourselves to molten spirits
And write their names with lava across our chests
And then
With sudden heart burns
Incurred from overloading on spiritual soul fool
We roar out a quilt of acid names
And
Shhhhhhhhhhhhhhhhhhhh
Listen
'Cause at this moment
(Which is all moments)
We hear a single name (Matt)
A sweat-lodge name that causes our maladies to perspire away
A tiger balm name that strengthens bones in the sauna of tradition
Matt Crawford
Doing Business As
A
Life lover/change maker/freedom dancer/dream enhancer/humble leader
Oppression hater/heart traveler/soul(full) radical/truth-giver/knowledge
  spreader
Root chiropractor/Juju spirit/Maasai warrior
Pain taker/love creator/fire maker
Son/father/husband/grandfather
Friend

To me

And you/and you

And we

And we sever vocal cords by yelling his name (Matt)

We tie-dye ku klux klan sheets with his righteousness (Matt)

We turn marijuana into sage

Cocaine into talcum powder

Crack into cowrie shells

And 40 ounces of malt liquor into wheat grass and aloe vera juice

With his scream for change (Matt)

We convert crips and bloods into new millennia griots and healers with his
memory (Matt)

We transform Republicans/Democrats/Independents/and unregistereds

Into communalists with his vocalized vision (Matt)

We make humans . . . worldly humanitarians with his smile and his laugh
(Matt)

And we make the 21st century a new universe(al) order with his heated heart
(Matt)

And when we are through making magic in the furnace of change

We hear his voice reverberate in our veins

And we feel our souls warm up

And we see him grin as we

FINALLY

Embrace the love tradition/the human mission

THE FIRE VISION

And our hearts become

Jimbes/and bongos/and congas/and darabukas/and tsuzumis

And timpanis/and naqqaras/and tom-toms/and tambourines/and 808s

And we hear Matt restfully beat the words

Well done

Well done

Well done

And we

Become the fire in the drum!!!

Let's All Take the Blame

"hey, we heard the news that someone's crying the blues
cause words still go unsaid while hungry minds are never fed"
                    —Earth, Wind and Fire, "Magic Mind"

"Slayings over popular items—sneakers, sunglasses, portable cassette
players—have occurred in recent years over the country, law enforcement
officials said. Leather jackets also have been a popular target."
                    —*Washington Post*, November 14, 1990

when black boys fondle their guns on TV &
shoot each other over storebought cowhide
when looks kill cause cocaine reigns &
anger drips acid on common sense
        let's all take the blame
let's all own up to somebody we've let down
some touch some praise we didn't give
        let's all admit
we've lunched on the widening Inspiration Gap
that got us thinking Black Life's not worth
the time it takes to say "nigger you better . . ."
        a. get out my face
        b. kiss my ass
        c. leave my woman alone
        d. all of the above
before settling the issue with
point-blank argument or automatic logic

        let's all take the blame
                feel the grief
                jerk from bullets in the heart
                recycle our own floorlength trinkets

I'm taking my own weight
I carry a heart around in my breast pocket
made of chipped rose quartz
a nick for each time
some High Noon Blood Notches his pistol
with another brother look like him
I'm looking no further than my own life
my own family & my own day-by-day connections
    I'm coating my conversations in peace
    I'm expanding my patience with justice
    I'm backing up my beliefs with courage

I have raised my blood pressure
but I ain't stressed out
coaxing magic into my voice
shifting opinions into shake & bake
dreaming soapbox-sized visions
praying in the privacy of demonstrations
wearing a psychic picket sign that says
    Black Life is more important

than   Nikes & Reeboks
      Toyotas & BMWs
      cellular phones & CD players
      Land Rovers & Blazers
      Bose speakers & beeper pagers

      Black Life is more important

than   vital national interests
      morale of U.S. troops overseas
      careers of mayors playing politics
      airing our dirty laundry in public
      reacting to slurs by Japanese politicians

Black Life is more important

than careers & MBAs
segmented marketing
expensive hotel conventions
demographic analysis
doomsday about the underclass

Black life is more important

than the Fresh Prince of Bel Air
the Jeffersons   the Evans
Cliff Huxtable Frank Parrish
Eddie Murphy making up with Spike Lee
Emmys & Oscars   Grammys & Tonys

Black Life is important
for more than we could ever earn 9 to 5
or buy Black   or boycott Korean
or haggle from vendors across from Cramton Auditorium
or along sidewalks on African Liberation Day

Black Life is important
for more even than
racial solidarity & class indifference
headshaking over the new generation
role models & gifts to our alma mater

Black Life is more than right reasons wrong reasons
Black Life is beyond any reasons at all
beyond the everyday & the unborn
beyond the past & the future
beyond the visible & the unseen
beyond the tears & the joy

Black Life is important, period.
Black Life is important, period.

Black Life is important
for more than we know
(more even than a gift from God)
for more than we will know
(more even than our ancestors' legacy)
Black Life is our planet
the balance between electrons & protons
the mystery of X & Y chromosomes
the gravity of black holes & quasars
Black Life is clean air & water
the cry of healthy babies
the freedom of reading & writing
the pleasure of breathing & laughter
the language of sex & love

Black Life is more even
than a gift from God
Black Life *is* God
period.

AMIRI BARAKA

Revelation in Brick City

Some time, on the street,
the dark begins to bite
you. If you stand and try to think
why wd dark bite, but then,
if you take it like it is,

and look around, clockers slanting,
drunk bro ranting, humanity scantly
recognizing its beginnings
under the madness of insanity
White America always been for us.

But try this, if you can
if you aint where the thugs have ran
translate your feelings into understanding,
And walk with that, keep it safe, and wake up
with that in your mind
in the morning.

Then work with that, and describe
yourself in that blunt mirror of actual
spiritual embezzlement

You can talk, out loud, to your self,
and accuse all and kill all
and return like Count Basie
from Monte Cristo, One More
Time.

as it be. You dig. Try that.

HAILE GERIMA

Sankofa

Spirit of the dead, rise up.
Lingering spirit of the dead, rise up and possess
your bird of passage.

Those stolen Africans step out of the ocean,
from the wombs of the ships and claim your story.

Spirit of the dead rise up, lingering spirit
of the dead rise up and possess your vessel.
Those Africans shackled and led, ironed
and enslaved step out of the acres of cane
fields and cotton fields and tell your story.

Spirit of the dead rise up, lingering spirits
of the dead rise up and possess your bird of
passage.

Those lynched in the magnolias, swinging
on the limbs of the weeping willows, rotting
food for the vultures step down and claim
your story.

Spirit of the dead rise up, lingering
spirits of the dead rise up and possess your
vessel.

Those tied, bound and whipped from
Brazil to Mississippi, step out and tell your
story.

Those in Jamaica, in the fields of Cuba,
in the swamps of Florida, the rice fields of
South Carolina, you waiting Africans step out
and tell your story.

Spirit of the dead rise up, lingering
spirit of the dead rise up and possess your
bird of passage

From Alabama to Suriname, up to the caves of
Louisiana, come out you African spirits, step
out and claim your stories.

You raped, slave-bred, castrated,
burned, tarred and feathered, roasted,
chopped, lobotomized, bound and gagged, you
African spirits,

Spirit of the dead rise up, lingering
spirit of the dead, rise up and possess your
bird of passage.

NIKKI GIOVANNI

But Since You Finally Asked

*(A Poem Commemorating the 10th Anniversary of the Slave Memorial at
Mount Vernon)*

No one asked us . . . what we thought of Jamestown . . . in
1619 . . . they didn't even say . . . "Welcome" . . . "You're
Home" . . . or even a pitiful . . . "I'm Sorry . . . But We Just
Can't Make It . . . Without You" . . . No . . . No one said a
word . . . They just snatched our drums . . . separated us by
language and gender . . . and put us on blocks . . . where our
beauty . . . like our dignity . . . was ignored

No one said a word . . . in 1776 . . . to us about Freedom . . .
The rebels wouldn't pretend . . . the British lied . . . We kept
to a space . . . where we owned our souls . . . since we understood . . . another century would pass . . . before we owned

our bodies . . . But we raised our voices . . . in a mighty cry
. . . to the Heavens above . . . for the strength to endure

No one says . . . "What I like about your people" . . . then
ticks off the wonder of the wonderful things . . . we've given
. . . Our song to God, Our strength to the Earth . . . Our un-
failing belief in forgiveness . . . I know what I like about us
. . . is that we let no one turn us around . . . not then . . . not
now . . . we plant our feet . . . on higher ground . . . I like who
we were . . . and who we are . . . and since someone has asked
. . . let me say: I am proud to be a Black American . . . I am
proud that my people labored honestly . . . with forbearance
and dignity . . . I am proud that we believe . . . as no other
people do . . . that all are equal in His sight . . . We didn't
write a constitution . . . we live one . . . We didn't say "We
the People" . . . we are one . . . We didn't have to add . . . as
an afterthought . . . "Under God" . . . We turn our faces to
the rising sun . . . knowing . . . a New Day . . . is always . . .
beginning

Jenoyne Adams is a fiction writer based in the Los Angeles area. She is currently completing her first novel.

Kwame Alexander is the author of *Just Us: Poems and Counter-poems* and the forthcoming children's book *That's My Daddy*. He is the CEO of the Alexander Publishing Group and the editor of the BlackWords Poetry Series. A graduate of Virginia Tech, he is the proud father of Nandi Assata Alexander.

Jabari Asim is the editor of *Eyeball*, a literary-arts journal. His fiction appears in *In the Tradition: An Anthology of Young Black Writers* and *Brotherman: The Odyssey of Black Men in America*. His poetry has appeared in *Black American Literature Forum, Obsidian II, Shooting Star Review*, and elsewhere. He has reviewed books for the St. Louis *Post-Dispatch, Los Angeles Times Book Review*, and *Emerge*, and he is currently an assistant editor at *The Washington Post Book World*.

Sabah As-Sabah was born and raised in Harlem, and died tragically at the young age of thirty. As a young revolutionary poet raised in the Islamic faith, Sabah produced, published, and performed a body of work that has left a lasting impression on poets of his generation, and poets to come. His voice lives on in such publications as *Sing, Eyeball, Nommo 2, Firewater Poetic, Poets and Writers Magazine, Release, American Letters and Commentary, The Road Before Us*, and the anthology *In the Tradition*. His book of poetry and prose, *Hail to the Holy Soul So Deep*, will be posthumously published.

Kupenda Auset (Joette Harland Watts) is a thirty-year-old poet and writer living in her hometown of Atlanta, Georgia. A graduate of Spelman College, she later attended Clark Atlanta University to work on a master's degree in Africana Women's Studies. Kupenda's work has appeared in several publications, including *In the Tradition: An Anthology of Young Black Writers, Catalyst,* and *Upscale* magazine. She is the author of the self-published *Life Poems: For Yesterday, Today, and Tomorrow.* Her second, forthcoming volume of poetry is entitled *Time Change.* Kupenda is the mother of Sakinah Nzinga Watts.

asha bandele is a poet and political activist who divides her time between New York and California. A cofounder of Black Star Express, her works appear in the anthologies *In the Tradition, Aloud,* and *In Defense of Mumia.* Her first collection of poetry, *Absence in the Palms of My Hands,* is published by Harlem River Press.

Amiri Baraka is a poet, dramatist, essayist, fiction writer, and political activist who is considered by many to be one of the most influential and preeminent literary figures of our time. Over the past thirty years, in addition to some thirteen volumes of poetry, he has produced over twenty plays, three jazz operas, seven volumes of nonfiction, and a novel. He has been awarded numerous literary prizes and honors, including an Obie Award for playwriting and the Langston Hughes Award from the City College of New York. He lives with his wife, the poet Amina Baraka, in his native city of Newark, New Jersey.

Nikkia Billingsley received an MFA in creative writing from Brooklyn College, where she studied with poets Laini Mataka and the late Allen Ginsberg. Currently she resides in her hometown of Los Angeles, California. Much of her writing draws humor and hope from the landscape and endless cast of characters in Los Angeles' streets. Her work has appeared in local and national magazines over the past three years.

Victor E. Blue is a graduate student in the history department at North Carolina Central University. As the descendant of African and Native American ancestors, he has emerged to give voice to the voiceless in his writings. A 1990 graduate of University of North Carolina's school of journalism, Victor has pursued graduate studies in Black Studies and Mass Communications. He has worked as a reporter for newspapers and wire services in North Carolina, Ohio, Indiana, and Illinois.

Mawiyah Kai El-Jamah Bomani is a twenty-four-year-old wife/mother/writer whose words have appeared in *FreeForm Magazine, Dark Eros,* and *Fertile Ground.*

Nadir Lasana Bomani is a New Orleans writer born and raised in the ninth ward. His works have appeared in *FreeForm Magazine, Dark Eros,* and *Fertile Ground.*

Charlie R. Braxton is a poet, playwright, and freelance journalist from McComb, Mississippi. His poems, essays, and reviews have appeared in a number of journals, including *The Black Nation, Black American Literature Forum, Cut Banks, Catalyst, Cross Roads, The Source, Vibe, Eyeball, Drum Voices Review,* and *The Minnesota Review.* His work has been anthologized in *In the Tradition, Soulfires, Word Up, Tough Love,* and *Trouble the Water.* Charlie's first volume of verse, *Ascension from the Ashes,* was published in 1990 by Blackwood Press. Currently he is working on a book about hip called *Reflections on Rap Music: From Bebop to Hip-Hop and It Don't Stop.*

Adwin Brown is a spoken-word/performance artist and composer. He is featured on the Bluezeum album *Portrait of a*

Groove and is the artistic director of the Peace & Fire performance group. He is the 1994 Lollapalooza Slam winner. Adwin is not afraid to eat asparagus, peanut butter, or bananas in public.

Elaine Brown is a former leading member of the Black Panther party. She is the author of the bestselling *A Taste of Power: A Black Woman's Story*. Elaine is president of a nonprofit organization called *Fields of Flowers*, which seeks to create a model alternative school for Black and poor children. She currently resides in Atlanta, Georgia, where she is working on a book tentatively entitled *Marching from Monticello: Racism in the New Age of William Jefferson Clinton*.

Kysha N. Brown is coeditor of *Fertile Ground 1996: Memories and Visions* and of the forthcoming *New Movements in Black Literature*. She is a member of NOMMO Literary Society in New Orleans, Louisiana.

Shonda Buchanan is a Los Angeles–based poet/writer and a graduate of Loyola Marymount University. She is the assistant editor for *Turning Point* magazine, as well as a contributing writer for the *LA Weekly* and *L.A. Times Magazine*. She is the recipient of the 1994 Brody Award in literature. Shonda published a chapbook entitled *strangefruitanickelamoon*. She is also the mother of a beautiful seven-year-old daughter named Afiya.

Beverly Fields Burnette is a native of Rocky Mount, North Carolina. She now works as a school social worker in Raleigh, North Carolina, and she enjoys combining her love of writing with the joy of serving people, especially children. In 1994 she self-published a chapbook of poems, *Searching for My Great-Grandmother at Stonewall and Other Poems*. Her poetry has been anthologized in *Adam of Ifé: Black Women in Praise of*

Black Men, Women's Words: A Journal of Carolina Writing, and in *Fertile Ground: Memories and Visions.* Her works in progress include a children's activity book, historical essays, and creative nonfiction.

Paul Calderón is a poet and member of the World Stage Anansi Writers' Workshop. His poetry has been performed at UCLA, UC-Davis, the Watts Towers, the International House of Blues, Luna Park, as well as other venues and festivals around and outside Los Angeles. He has been the opening act for the rap group Cypress Hill, as well as written and performed two radio commercials for Nike. Paul is currently working on a degree in Philosophy at UCLA and plans on continuing his career in poetry, fiction, song lyrics, philosophy, film, and television.

Kenneth Carroll is a native Washingtonian whose poetry and plays have appeared in *Black Literature Forum, Catalyst Magazine, African Commentary, NOMMO, Konch Magazine, Hungry As We Are, Fast Talk Full Volume, In Search of Color Everywhere,* and *Spirit and Flame.* His latest book of poetry is entitled *So What: For the White Dude Who Said This Ain't Poetry.* Kenneth is the D.C. Site Coordinator for WritersCorps, an arts and social-service program founded by the NEA and Americorps. He is also the proud father of a teenage son.

Ta-Nehisi (pronounced Tah-Nah-Ha-See) **Coates** was born and raised in Baltimore, Maryland. He is currently attending Howard University, pursuing an undergraduate degree in History. Ta-Nehisi is the winner of the Larry Neal award for poetry and is also a staff writer for the *Washington CityPaper.* His poetry appeared in the anthology *Testimony.* He credits Robert Hayden, Larry Neal, Zora Neale Hurston, Rakim, and his parents as his primary literary influences. He is the author of the chapbook *Asphalt Sketches.*

Chuck D is the leader and cofounder of one of the most-talked-about rap groups ever, Public Enemy. Chuck has parlayed a booming voice, congenial yet forceful personality, and the articulation skills necessary to present often inflammatory viewpoints into a hugely successful performance style and much-imitated empire. As a theorist, lyricist, and head rapper, he's quoted constantly, seen on television around the planet, and idolized by legions of youth from all backgrounds. He recently published a book entitled *Fight the Power: Rap, Race, and Reality* and is an analyst and news correspondent for the Fox News Channel.

Kamau Daáood is a performance poet, educator, and community arts activist who is a native of Los Angeles. A former member of the Watts Writers' Workshop, he is the subject of an award-winning documentary film, *Life Is a Saxophone,* and the author of two chapbooks of poetry. Kamau, along with world-renowned master drummer Billy Higgins founded the World Stage Performance Gallery, and he is one of the architects of the arts movement in the Leimert Park area of Los Angeles. His most recent work is a poetry/spoken-word CD entitled *Leimert Park.*

Michael Datcher was born in 1967 on Chicago's south side and raised on the east side of Long Beach, California. While a student at the University of California at Berkeley, he edited the national black men's poetry anthology, *My Brother's Keeper.* After graduating from Berkeley in 1992, he began his master's degree in African-American Literature at UCLA. His essays and articles have appeared in *Vibe,* the *L.A. Times, The Baltimore Sun, Buzz,* and the anthologies *Testimony: Young African Americans on Self-Discovery and Black Identity* and *Soulfires: Young Black Men on Love and Violence.* He is coordinator and host of the critically acclaimed World Stage Anansi Writers' Workshop in Los Angeles' Crenshaw district.

Derrick X (Goldie Williams) (a.k.a. Goldie the Poet) is a Bay Area native who has been diligently crafting poetry and prose since his early adolescence. His adroit command of his talent has been rewarded with an opening slot for singer/songwriter Me'Shell Ndege 'Ocello; appearances at Atlanta's renowned annual Black Arts Festival; and touring with fellow poet D-Knowledge. He is also an actor who scored a feature role in the infamous mini-movie *Murder Was the Case,* directed by Dr. Dre and starring Snoop Doggy Dog. Goldie imbues his artistic endeavor with a strong sense of truth, striving to impart hope to all those who genuinely strive for love, peace, and understanding.

Toi Derricotte was born in Detroit, Michigan. She has published four collections of poetry, *Natural Birth; The Empress of the Death House; Captivity,* which is in its fourth printing; and most recently, *Tender.* Her latest book is a literary memoir, *The Black Notebooks.* Her poems have appeared in many magazines and journals, including *American Poetry Review, The Iowa Review, Callaloo, The Paris Review, Ploughshares, The Kenyon Review, The Massachusetts Review,* and in numerous anthologies. She is an associate professor of English at the University of Pittsburgh, and she has taught in the graduate creative writing programs at New York University, George Mason University, and Old Dominion University.

Bill Duke is a native of Poughkeepsie, New York, and was educated at Boston University and NYU's Tisch School of the Arts. He is a director, producer, writer, and actor involved in film, theater, television, literature, the Internet, drama, comedy, and inspiration. You name the creative act, and Bill's done it—always with the same devotion to integrity, quality, and great entertainment. He has directed *Rage in Harlem, Deep*

Cover, *The Cemetery Club*, *Sister Act 2: Back in the Habit*, and most recently *Hoodlum*.

Haile Gerima was born in Gondor, Ethiopia. As a youth, Haile performed in his father's theater troupe, which presented original and often historical drama, always immersed in the genuine culture of Ethiopia. Gerima came to the United States in 1967 to study at Chicago's Goodman School of Drama. He slowly realized that "with cinema I could control many more things than in the theater." Haile went on to receive his MFA from UCLA in 1976 and is currently on sabbatical as a tenured professor of film at Howard University. With the release of *Sankofa* and six other feature-length films, as well as awards and participation in a host of various international film festivals, Haile has gained international acclaim and is considered a torchbearer for the burgeoning independent African and African-American film movement.

Brian Gilmore was born and raised in Washington, D.C., where he still lives, works, and writes. He is an attorney, poet, and author of a collection of poems entitled *elvis presley is alive and well and living in harlem*. His work has appeared in *The Nation*, *The Washington Afro-America*, *In Search of Color Everywhere*, *Black Books Bulletin*, *The Unity Line*, *Mondo Elvis*, *Fast Talk*, *Full Volume*, *Soulfires*, *Obsidian II*, and *The Drumming Between Us*.

Nikki Giovanni is the author of thirteen books of poetry, including *Black Feeling Black Talk/Black Judgement*, *Re:Creation*, *My House*, *The Women and the Men*, *Cotton Candy on a Rainy Day*, *Those Who Ride the Night Wind*, and *The Selected Poems of Nikki Giovanni*. She has also published the essay collections *Sacred Cows . . . and Other Edibles* and *Racism 101*, and two colloquies, *A Dialogue: James Baldwin and Nikki Giovanni* and *A Poetic Equation: Conversations Between Nikki*

Giovanni and Margaret Walker. Named Woman of the Year by *Mademoiselle, Ladies' Home Journal,* and *Essence,* Nikki reads her poetry all the over the country and holds thirteen honorary doctoral degrees. She is a professor of English at Virginia Polytechnic.

Eddie Griffin is a comedian and actor who currently stars on the television show *Malcolm and Eddie.*

M. Eliza Hamilton is of Fulani (Guinea), Jamaican, Grenadian, and Carib Indian ancestry. She has a self-published chapbook *What Is Now Unanswerable,* and has been published in several anthologies. She is currently working on a second collection of poems.

Duriel E. Harris is a native of Chicago who now lives in New York City and teaches at the Dalton School. She is a cofounder of The Language Art Collective and is presently working on a manuscript. Her poems have most recently been published in *Spirit and Flame: An Anthology of Contemporary African-American Poetry.*

Peter J. Harris is the founding publisher/editor of *The Drumming Between Us: Black Love & Erotic Poetry,* a Los Angeles magazine, and author of *Hand Me My Griot Clothes: The Autobiography of Junior Baby.* His fiction has been published in the bestselling anthology *Breaking Ice,* edited by Terry McMillan. Harris's poetry has been published in *In Search of Color Everywhere,* edited by E. Ethelbert Miller, and *I Hear a Symphony: African Americans Celebrate Love,* edited by Paula Woods and Felix Lidell.

Yona Harvey is originally from Cincinnati, Ohio. She is currently a student at Howard University, majoring in English, with a double minor in Art and Spanish. Yona's poetry has been featured in *Janus* (Howard's student literary journal), and she was awarded an honorable mention in the John C. Wright poetry contest. She has also contributed a "poetic interlude" to Flatline Comics' "Flatbush Native."

Defari Herut earned his BA at the University of California, Berkeley, and his MA from Columbia University. In addition to being a hip-hop artist and member of the Likwit Crew, he is a high-school teacher at Inglewood High School in Southern California.

Jamal is a poet, photographer, and a self-proclaimed "family man." Jamal received his BA from the University of California, Berkeley, and is currently a special-education high-school teacher in Los Angeles.

Wendy L. James is the recipient of the 1997 Brody Award for literature. She has taught poetry and creative writing throughout Los Angeles and is a program director for various nonprofit organizations. She recently published a chapbook entitled *Deliverance*.

Honorée F. Jeffers was reared in Durham, North Carolina. She holds a BA in English Literature from Talladega College and an MFA in Creative Writing from the University of Alabama. She has studied with poets Lenard D. Moore, Toi Derricotte, Cornelius Eady, Lyn Hejinian, and the scholar/poet Jerry Ward, Jr. Honorée's poetry deals with issues of feminism, blackness, and voice, and like her father, poet Lance F. Jeffers, she believes that the writing of any poem should involve both an artistic and political process, and that the primary goal of art is liberation.

Candice M. Jenkins is a twenty-two-year-old poet, artist, and photographer who believes in the transformative power of both love and literature. She is a proud graduate of Spelman College and is currently pursuing her Ph.D. in English from Duke University. Her work has been published in *Cymbals, Red Clay,* and *Black Arts Quarterly.*

June Jordan is a political activist and award-winning poet and essayist. She is the recipient of the 1995 Lila Wallace–Reader's Digest Writer's Award and the author of over twenty books, including *Civil Wars, Technical Difficulties, Haruko/Love Poems,* and the libretto *I Was Looking at the Ceiling and Then I Saw the Sky.* A frequent contributor to *The Progressive,* June is a professor of African-American Studies and Women's Studies at the University of California, Berkeley.

Glenn Joshua is a founding member of the New Orleans–based Nommo Literary Society, and is a performer with the Word Band Featuring Kalamu Ya Salaam. His short stories have been published in the anthology *Fertile Ground.* Joshua is also a professional firefighter who currently resides in New Orleans.

Kalunda-rae is originally from New York. Currently she is a creative writing student at the University of Southern California.

Mendi Lewis is a poet, musician, and graduate student in Literature at Duke University. Her work has been published in *Black Arts Quarterly, Amethyst,* and *Focus Literary Magazine.*

John W. Love, Jr., is a native and resident of Charlotte, North Carolina. His visionary work in the performing arts, visual arts, and the literary arts has taken him all over the world. As he continues to traverse the infinite dimensionality of the vessels that embody his creativity, in an easy awe, he continues to cherish the whispers of those who are unseen.

K. Curtis Lyle is a founding member of the famed Watts Writers' Workshop. He has taught, lectured, and read his poetry in the major intellectual and urban centers of North America. He is committed to restoring poetry to the forefront of the performing and ritual arts. Currently, he lives in Oakland, California.

Anthony C. Lyons, Sr., is a Los Angeles native. He is a novelist, poet, short-story writer, and cofounder of the Anansi Writers' Workshop. At present, he supports his family as either a computer programmer or systems engineer. He is currently working on his second novel entitled *Pearls.*

Haki R. Madhubuti is a poet, essayist, critic, and founder of Third World Press. An influential African-American poet, Haki has published several books, including *Think Black; Don't Cry; Scream;* and *We Walk the Way of the New World;* as well as *Black Men: Obsolete, Single, Dangerous?* and *Why L.A. Happened: Implications of the '92 Los Angeles Rebellion.* He was one of the leading figures of the Black Arts movement and continues to be active in the promotion of the arts.

Sonja Marie earned a BA in Theater Arts from Hampton University. Sonja has worked with such artists as Kenneth "Babyface" Edmonds, Chanté Moore, Patrice Rushen, and Tony Rich. One of her greatest achievements thus far has been as a performer and one of three writers featured on the multiplatinum album *Waiting to Exhale.*

Keith Antar Mason is a poet, playwright, artist, community activist, and creator of the Hittite Empire, an African-American male performance-art collective that has performed throughout the world.

Tony Medina teaches English at Long Island University's Brooklyn campus, New York University, and at Borough of Manhattan Community College, CUNY. He is the literature editor of

NOBBO: A Journal of African American Dialogue. He is also the author of *No Noose Is Good Noose, Haiku d'État, Follow Up Letters to Santa from Kids Who Never Got a Response, Cantos for the Comatose,* and coeditor of *In Defense of Mumia.* Tony's work is featured in the anthologies *In the Tradition, Aloud, Soulfires, Tough Love, Spirit & Flame,* and *Identity Lessons,* as well as many literary and popular-culture publications. Tony also played a significant role in the production of this anthology.

E. Ethelbert Miller is an editor for various literary publications, including *The African-American Review,* and the author of eight books of poetry. He is a board member of the PEN/ Faulkner Foundation and the director of the African-American Resource Center at Howard University. He is also the editor of *In Search of Color Everywhere: A Collection of African-American Poetry.*

Lenard D. Moore was born on February 13, 1958, in Jacksonville, North Carolina, and graduated magna cum laude with a BA degree from Shaw University. He is the founder and executive director of the Carolina African American Writers' Collective, and has been published in numerous magazines and anthologies. He is the author of *Desert Storm: A Brief History* and *Forever Home* and was twice awarded the Haiku Museum of Tokyo Award. A former writer-in-residence for the United Arts Council of Raleigh and Wake County, he is the chairman of the North Carolina Haiku Society.

Lynn G. Moore is a student at Shaw University and works for the North Carolina Department of Education. She is also a proud wife and mother.

Maiisha L. Moore was born on May 30, 1982, in Raleigh, North Carolina, the daughter of Lenard D. Moore and Lynn

G. Moore. She was elected to membership in the National Junior Beta Club and in the spring of 1996 was selected an All-American Scholar by the United States Achievement Academy. She has also won numerous awards for track and field. She loves art and reading.

Lana Moorer (a.k.a. MC Lyte) is a pioneering female rapper—her single "Ruffneck" was the first gold record for a female hip-hop artist. Raised in Brooklyn and Queens, she has been rapping since she was twelve-years-old and has been cited as a major influence for many young artists, both male and female. Lyte's music has been recognized for not resorting to the caricature-like posturing that has plagued other rappers, as well as for its anti-violence message. She also contributes to social efforts and programs that are important to her, such as Rock the Vote and the fight against AIDS. She is currently working on a children's book, various acting endeavors, and her sixth album.

Merilene M. Murphy is the poet-author of *Under Peace Rising*. Merilene is perhaps best known for founding the global poetry performance venue Telepoetics, which has been exchanging live poetry events to and from Los Angeles via videophone since 1991.

Letta Simone-Nefertari Neely was born and raised in Indiana and currently lives in Harlem, New York. She is the author of two chapbooks and was the recipient of a 1994 New York Foundation of the Arts grant.

Art Nixon lives in the Los Feliz section of Hollywood, California. He has published poetry and essays in various journals, including *Ju-Ju: Research Papers in Afro-American Studies*, and *Black American Literature Forum*. He has a BA in American Studies from Case Western Reserve University and is a member of the Los Angeles–based Organization of Black Screen-writers.

V. Kali Nurigan is a mother, calligrapher, and creator of Venéla's Vegetarian Soul. She loves, lives, and breathes in Los Angeles.

Ojenke was born in 1947 in the city of Los Angeles. He is a founding member of the Watts Writers' Workshop. Ojenke has performed his poetry throughout the country and is the inspiration for many of L.A.'s young poets.

Oktavi has performed as a featured reader in the greater Los Angeles area and has participated in the California Arts Council, Artist-in-Communities Residency program. While in California, she was one of the founding members of the women's writing group Motley Cabal and founding editor of *Teen View*, a Los Angeles newsletter for young writers. She is currently a member of the Carolina African-American Writers' Collective. Oktavi has published a collection of poems entitled *Restoration*. Although her main focus is poetry, she is currently working on several short fiction pieces. Oktavi is a New York native who resides with her daughter, Rebecca, in Durham, North Carolina.

Shaquille O'Neal is the star center for the Los Angeles Lakers. He is also a multiplatinum recording artist, actor, philanthropist, and successful businessman.

Abiodun Oyewole is an original member of the legendary group The Last Poets. He is a playwright, songwriter, community activist, and poet who enjoys bringing out the poetry in all people's lives. Currently he lives in New York City, where he teaches poetry at Columbia University, conducts several creative-writing workshops, and is a consultant for the Board of Education. He has performed his poetry around the world and is considered by many to be one of the fathers of rap/hip-hop.

Poetri is a Los Angeles–based writer, poet, actor, and the co-owner of RAZZOP Productions. With God at the helm of his life, Poetri knows that there is no obstacle he cannot overcome. His production company has composed, produced, and arranged over eighty television and radio commercials, including several commercials for Nike in which he utilized poets and rappers from around the country.

Kevin Powell is perhaps best known as a cast member on MTV's *Real World*. He was a senior writer at *Vibe* magazine for three years and is the coeditor (with Ras Baraka) of *In the Tradition: An Anthology of Young Black Writers*. Kevin's first volume of poetry, *recognize*, was published in 1995. His latest work is a book of letters entitled *Keepin' It Real: Post-MTV Reflections on Race, Sex, and Politics.*

Rohan B. Preston is the winner of the 1997 Henry Blakely, Jr., Poetry Prize and the recipient of a 1996 fellowship from the Illinois Arts Council. Rohan authored the poetry collection *Dreams in Soy Sauce* and coedited the multigenre anthology *Soulfires: Young Black Men on Love and Violence*. His forthcoming book is an appraisal of the current, century-capping surge in Black artistic expression. His poems have appeared in, among other publications, *The Atlanta Review, The Crab Orchard Review, Eyeball, Hammers, Ploughshares, River Styx,* and *TriQuarterly.*

Eric Priestley is a founding member of the Watts Writers' Workshop who has performed his poetry on almost every continent. He is the 1997 winner of the Pacificas Foundation Literary Prize, and he recently completed two novels, *National*

Security and *Shorty Blue.* Eric has also written poetry in French and Spanish, and he is beginning to write in German and several African dialects.

DJ Renegade (Joel Dias-Porter) was born and raised in Pittsburgh, PA. After high school he enlisted in the USAF as a computer operator, and upon leaving the service, he spent the next eight years as a professional disk jockey in D.C. area nightclubs. In 1991 he quit his job and began living in homeless shelters, where he began seriously writing and performing poetry. He has performed his work on the *Today* show, in a commercial for Legal Jeans, in the video documentary *Voices Against Violence,* and on BET's *Teen Summit.* Currently based in Washington, D.C., he is a member of WriterCorps.

El Rivera was born in Harlem at the crest of a wave. She was reared as a ward of the state of Maryland. Upon turning twenty-one, El relocated to Los Angeles, California, where she continues to reside. El considers herself a performance poet. She believes that the only permanence is change and that sincere efforts are rewarded.

Roland Poet X (Roland Hayes Porter, Jr.) is a Native of Detroit, Michigan, where he was a member of Detroit's Black Panther party. Roland is a poet, filmmaker, and community activist who uses God's tools to fight the devil's racism.

Sonia Sanchez is a poet, mother, activist, and professor. Sonia is the author of fifteen books, including *Homecoming, We a BaddDDD People, Love Poems, I've Been a Woman: New and Selected Poems, Sound Investment and Other Stories, Homegirls and Handgrenades, Under a Soprano Sky, Wounded in the House of a Friend,* and most recently, *Does Your House Have Lions?* Sonia has lectured at over five hundred universities and colleges in the United States and has traveled extensively, reading her poetry in Africa, Cuba, England, the Caribbean, Australia, Nicaragua, the People's Republic of China, Norway, and Canada. She was the first Presidential Fellow at Temple University and she holds the Laura Carnell Chair in English at Temple University.

Ntozake Shange is a poet, dramatist, and author of the famous choreopoem *for colored girls who have considered suicide when the rainbow is enuf,* which opened on Broadway in 1976. This piece won an Obie Award and was nominated for an Emmy, Grammy, and Tony. Shange currently resides in Philadelphia, but she is an artist of the world.

Angela Shannon is a poet whose works have appeared in *The Crab Orchard Review, Jackleg, Ploughshares, TriQuarterly, The Willow Review,* and Dr. Lewis Gordon's *Black Text and Black Textuality: Deconstructing Blackness,* among other publications. Her poems also appear in E. Ethelbert Miller's *Beyond the Frontier.* She is the winner of the 1997 Willow Review Poetry Prize as well as a 1996 poetry award from the Illinois Arts Council. Angela is a member of the Chicago-based Blue Ellipsis Collective. Currently she is completing *Rootwomen,* her inaugural poetry collection.

Glenis Redmond Sherer was a clinical counselor and a family counselor in her former life. She is now on roster as an artist with the South Carolina Arts Commission in literature and poetry. She is a member of the Asheville Poetry Slam Team, which won the Asheville Poetry Festival Slam in 1995 and 1996. Her first chapbook was funded by a grant from the Metropolitan Arts Council from the Arthur and Holly McGill Fund. Her chapbook is entitled *NAMING IT!*

Evelyn E. Shockley is originally from Chicago and is currently a Ph.D. student at Duke University. She is a recent member of the Carolina African-American Writers' Collective. She lives in Durham, North Carolina.

Patricia Smith is an award-winning journalist, poet, playwright, and performer. Patricia is a four-time national individual champion of the notorious and wildly popular poetry slam. She is the author of *Close to Death* and *Big Towns, Big,* as well as being published in *The Paris Review, TriQuarterly, AGNI,* and other literary journals. A Metro columnist for *The Boston Globe,* Patricia also worked for the *Chicago Sun-Times* as an arts critic and investigative reporter.

Speech is best known as the lead vocalist/songwriter for the group Arrested Development, and is also known for his unique and fresh "Life Music" which crashed upon an unexpecting music world in 1992. In 1995 he released his first self-titled solo effort to critical acclaim. Currently Speech is completing his next solo album, entitled *1998 Hoopla.*

Christopher Stanard was born in Washington, D.C., and raised in Charlotte, North Carolina. He has earned degrees from Morehouse College and Georgia Tech. His poetry has appeared in *Spirit and Flame.* He is a member of the Carolina African-American Writers' Collective.

Cree Summer is originally from Saskatchewan, Canada, and was raised on the Red Feasant Reservation. She is a friend to fairies all over the world. Along with Lilakoi Moon, she is the creator of a poetry venue called The Circle. Cree says she "came to L.A. to be a star . . . be careful what you ask for, because you might not be able to get rid of it."

Mariahadessa "Ekere" Tallie is a New York–based poet and writer. Her work has been published in *African Voices, Eyeball,* and the *Atlanta Bulletin.* She is currently working on a novel.

Cheryl Boyce Taylor is a Trinidadian poet whose work has been featured in *ALOUD: Nuyorican Poets Anthology*, *The Maryland Poetry Review*, and *In Defense of Mumia*. She earned her BA in Theater along with master's degrees in Education and Social Work. Her twenty-year foundation as a poet includes studies with Audre Lorde, June Jordan, and Molly Peacock.

Lisa B. Thompson is a native of San Francisco, California. This poet, playwright, essayist, and performance artist received both her BA in English Literature and her MA in African-American Studies from UCLA. She is currently enrolled in Stanford University's doctoral program in Modern Thought and Literature, where she is studying contemporary African-American literature, film, and performance. She is working on a collection of poetry and short stories about growing up as a black woman in the Bay Area during the seventies.

Chezia Thompson-Cager, a poet and playwright from St. Louis, Missouri, is the author of *Presence of Things Unseen: Giant Talk* and the recipient of the Artscape '96 Literary Arts Award for poetry. She teaches at the Maryland Institute College of Art and is an adviser for the Carolina African-American Writers' Collective. She lives in Baltimore, Maryland.

T'Kalla is a poet and activist based in Brooklyn, New York. He is the cofounder of Black Star Express, a poetry collective with chapters in New York City and Oakland, California. He is also a member of the Vibe Chameleons. In 1994 T'Kalla directed an independent film, *Big Crew,* which documents some of the poets in the current New York underground. He recently completed his first book of poetry and prose entitled *Raising Sugarkane!*

A. K. Toney is a poet, writer, and performance artist. He is a member of the Anansi Writers' Workshop. A. K. is also a mem-

ber of the Hittite Empire (an all African-American male performance art group), and has traveled extensively with them since
1993 across the nation. He is also a founder and member of
the performance art group known as the Ibeji Players, who
have performed in Los Angeles and have lectured at California
Institute of the Arts. A. K. describes his poetry as urban vernacular slang that rides along the rhythms of hip-hop culture.

Askia M. Touré is a poet, essayist, editor, and political activist
who is one of the architects and leading voices of the Black
Arts movement. He is a former editor of *The Journal of Black
Poetry, Black Dialogue & Black Star,* as well as a staff writer
for *Liberator* magazine. Askia has been published in a host of
anthologies in the United States and abroad. He is the author
of *Ju-Ju, Songhai!,* and *From the Pyramids to the Projects,* volumes of verse, and coauthor of *Samory Touré,* a political biog-
raphy.

Quincy Troupe is the winner of two American Book Awards, a
Peabody Award, and the title of World Heavyweight Champion
Poet. Quincy was a featured poet on Bill Moyers's PBS television special *The Power of the Word.* He is the author of a
number of poetry books, and is also the editor of *James Baldwin: The Legacy* and coauthor of the bestseller *Miles: The Autobiography.* A longtime resident of New York, Quincy now
lives in California, where he is a professor of literature and
creative writing at the University of California, San Diego.

Mario Van Peebles is a director, producer, actor, and, most recently, author. His feature-film-directing debut, the critically
acclaimed *New Jack City* and his controversial *Panther,* as well
as his breakthrough multicultural western, *Posse,* have established him as one of the most distinguished young film direc-
tors in the country. His most recent film projects include *Los
Locos* and *Love Kills.* He received a degree in Economics from

Columbia University and was also awarded a Doctor of Humane Letters degree from Hofstra University.

Dr. Madd Vibe, (a.k.a. the Missin' Link) can be found on the left elbow of Angelo Moore. He was originally born in the City of Lost Assholes from undisputed, much-loved Ma and Pa Johnson & Moore on November 5, 1965. In 1985, he began his career as a Scientist of Fishbone Musicology. After receiving his first doctorate degree at the University of Comprehensive Linkology, he was pronounced the Missin' Link, the Incomparable, the good Dr. Madd Vibe.

Roni Walter was born in Biloxi, Mississippi, and currently resides in Los Angeles, California. She is the creator of Roni'z Bakstreet Poetri, which has provided numerous poets with a venue to perform poetry. She describes her work as southern-jazzy, hip-hop poetry. Roni has performed her poetry at the House of Blues, The Comedy Store, and at various venues in and outside of Los Angeles. Her poetry has also been performed by singer/actress Brandi on the sitcom *Moesha*. Roni dedicates all her work to God, her mama, and to Roni'z Backstreet Kidz.

Michael War's awards for poetry include an NEA Creative Writing Fellowship and the Gwendolyn Brooks Significant Illinois Poets Award. He is author of the poetry collection *We Are All the Black Boy* and the unpublished manuscript *Hero Worship,* and his poems have been widely anthologized. He is executive director of the Guild Complex, an award-winning cross-cultural literary center. In 1996 he was awarded an Entrepreneur of the Year in the Arts Award from Columbia College.

Jerry W. Ward, Jr., is a highly respected literary critic. He is the coauthor of *Black Southern Voices* with John O Killens and is the editor of *Trouble the Waters: 250 Years of Black Poetry.* His poetry and essays have appeared in various journals. He is a professor at Tougaloo College in Tougaloo, Mississippi.

Pam Ward is a Los Angeles native and graphic designer. She likes to write about all that stuff your mother told you hush, when you asked her: violence, strife, and long rides on the jacked-up concrete of L.A. She's worked the hash-food line in high school, the fry machine at Mickie Dee's, and did temp work for two sex maniacs before starting her own business, Ward Graphics. She has been published in *Grand Passion,* an anthology of Los Angeles Poets, has received a poetry award from *New Letters Magazine,* University of Missouri Press, and recently received a *California Arts Council Fellowship* for poetry. She is the editor of the literary journal *Picasso's Mistress.*

Malcolm-Jamal Warner is a multitalented artist. Many people first became aware of him in his role as Bill Cosby's son, Theo, on *The Cosby Show.* Currently Malcolm is the star of the sitcom *Malcolm and Eddie.* He is a screenwriter, director, and a poet who is very active in the Los Angeles poetry scene.

Paula White-Jackson is an award-winning poet. Her poetry has appeared in *Obsidian II* among other publications. She is a member of the Carolina Writers' Collective and is currently living in Asheborough, North Carolina.

Crystal A. Williams is originally from Detroit, Michigan, and now resides in Staten Island, New York. She began her poetry career at the Nuyorican Poets Café, where she became the captain of the 1995 New York Slam Team. Since her first performance in New York in 1994, Crystal has performed at many of the country's premiere venues, including the Whitney Museum of American Art, the Smithsonian, and on *It's Showtime at the Apollo.* She is currently working on a memoir, a manuscript of poetry, and a second one-woman show.

Karen Williams, poet, essayist, and freelance editor/writer, is also a health administrator in metro Detroit. A Detroit Black Writers' Guild member, she has studied with poets Toi Derricotte, Lawrence Joseph, and playwright Ron Milner. Williams received her BSJ degree from Ohio University, and a master's degree in English Education from Detroit's Wayne State University. Her poetry has been published in *Spirit and Flame: A Contemporary Anthology of African-American Poetry, Poetry Motel, Silver Wings,* and *Midwest Poetry Review,* among other anthologies and journals.

Lana C. Williams is originally from Detroit, Michigan. She is a staff writer for the *Independent Weekly* and has published her poetry in *Fertile Ground* and *African-American Review.* Lana is associate editor of *New Visions Literary Review.* She is cofounder of LaJan Production and is president of the Carolina African-American Writers' Collective. She lives in Cary, North Carolina.

Marlon C. Williams (PoetX) is a graduate of Georgia Tech University who frequents Atlanta's underground poetry circuit. Son of light, blood brother of rhythm, author of *VERSATILITY, Verse Art-Illery Is What I Give 'Em.* Rhymes rocks tunes like moonlit liquid floaters, Poetx the paper vapor maker, Souljah awakener, sensual Sister soul soaker.

Niama Leslie Williams was born and raised in Los Angeles, California. She is a writer, scholar, and adjunct professor who is particularly concerned with the emotional survival of her people. She teaches African-American Literature, with an emphasis on spirituality. She is also a doctoral student in African-American Studies at Temple University.

Saul Stacey Williams was born in Newburgh, New York, and currently resides in Brooklyn. Saul received a BA in Philosophy and Drama from Morehouse University and an MFA in Acting from New York University. He is the 1996 Grand Slam Champion for the Nuyorican Poets Café. He has published two chapbooks, *Untimely Meditations* and *Children of the Night*. His poetry is featured in the documentary *Underground Voices* and the album *Eargasms*.

A(e)rin Wilson is a nonsmoking graduate student in New York City. She was born between the ocean and a field of strawberries in 1973 and has been published in various journals and newspapers since this event. A(e)rin is a recovering television addict, taking it one day at a time.

Kalamu Ya Salaam is a New Orleans writer and arts producer/administrator. His latest books are *The Magic of JuJu: An Appreciation of the Black Arts Movement* and a travel book, *Tarzan Can Not Return to Africa, But I Can*. His latest spoken-word CD is *My Story, My Song*. He is the founder of the Nommo Literary Society and coeditor/publisher of *Fertile Ground*, a Black literary annual.

281

Brian Gilmore: "Hazing." Copyright © 1996 by Brian Gilmore. Reprinted by permission of the author.

Nikki Giovanni: "But Since You Finally Asked," from *The Selected Poems of Nikki Giovanni* (William Morrow and Company). Copyright © 1996 by Nikki Giovanni. Reprinted by permission of the author.

Wendy L. James: "Troy," from *Deliverance* (The Inevitable Press). Copyright © 1997 by Wendy L. James. Reprinted by permission of the author.

John W. Love, Jr.: "Moment 9/The Woman," from the play *Picture Perfect Images from the Mocha Regions of a Chocolate Boy's Reality*. Copyright © 1991 by John W. Love, Jr.

McLyte: "Everyday," from *Bad as I Wanna B.* copyright © 1996 by East-West. All rights reserved. Reprinted with permission.

Haki R. Madhubuti: "A Bonding," from *Black Men: Obsolete, Single, Dangerous?* (Third World Press). Copyright © 1990 by Haki R. Madhubuti. Reprinted by permission of the author.

E. Ethelbert Miller: "Mountain Wife," from *phati'tude*, Vol. 1, No. 1/Spring 1997. Copyright © 1997 by E. Ethelbert Miller. Reprinted by permission of the author.

Lenard D. Moore: "a black woman," from *The Open Eye* (The North Carolina Haiku Society Press). Copyright © 1985 by Lenard D. Moore. Reprinted by permission of the author.

Maiisha L. Moore: "the dark rock-road," from *Holiday Haiku* (The North Carolina Haiku Society Press). Copyright © 1990 by Maiisha L. Moore. Reprinted by permission of the author.

282

INDEX OF CONTRIBUTORS

Adams, Jenoyne, 109–111
Alexander, Kwame, 235
Asim, Jabari, 234
As-Sabah, Sabah, 102–103, 240–241
Auset, Kupenda (Joette Harland Watts), 123–125

bandele, asha, 32–36
Baraka, Amiri, 8, 57–61, 62, 249–250
Billingsley, Nikkia, 19–20
Blue, Victor E., 15
Bomani, Mawiyah Kai El-Jamah, 79–80
Bomani, Nadir Lasana, 87–88, 168
Braxton, Charlie R., 41–42
Brown, Adwin, 169–170
Brown, Elaine, 20–25
Brown, Kysha N., 128
Buchanan, Shonda, 114–115
Burnette, Beverly Fields, 69

Calderón, Paul, 177–180
Carroll, Kenneth, 8–11
Coates, Ta-nehisi, 173–174

D, Chuck, 152–154
Daáood, Kamau, 43–45
Datcher, Michael, 115–123
Derrick X (a.k.a. Goldie the Poet), 125–126
Derricotte, Toi, 63–64
Duke, Bill, 46–48

Gerima, Haile, 250–252
Gilbert, Derrick I. M. (a.k.a. D-Knowledge), xiii–xxiii, 3–7, 48–50, 57–60, 95–97, 145, 147–148, 191–193, 221–223, 230–232, 243–245
Gilmore, Brian, 78–79

Giovanni, Nikki, 252–253
Griffin, Eddie, 168–169

Hamilton, M. Eliza, 81–82
Harris, Duriel E., 127
Harris, Peter J., 246–249
Harvey, Yona, 241–242
Herut, Defari, 204–205

Jamal, 106–107
James, Wendy L., 107
Jeffers, Honorée F., 131
Jenkins, Candice M., 210–211
Jordan, June, 3–7, 51–53
Joshua, Glenn, 134

Kalunda-rae, 16–19

Lewis, Mendi, 203–204
Love, John W., Jr., 181–183
Lyle, K. Curtis, 103–105
Lyons, Anthony C., 112–114

Madhubuti, Haki R., 90–91
Marie, Sonja, 238–239
Mason, Keith Antar, 11–12
Medina, Tony, 58–60, 162–167, 221
Miller, E. Ethelbert, 80–81
Moore, Lenard D., 77
Moore, Lynn G., 77
Moore, Maiisha L., 78
Moorer, Lana (a.k.a. MC Lyte), 139
Murphy, Merilene M., 73–76

Neely, Letta Simone-Nefertari, 25–32
Nixon, Art, 199–201
Nurigan, V. Kali, 88–90

Ojenke, 141
Oktavi, 159–160

O'Neal, Shaquille, 83–87
Oyewole, Abiodun, 145–148, 149–150, 185–187

Poetri, 161
Powell, Kevin, 36–41
Preston, Rohan B., 67–68
Priestley, Eric, 236–237

Renegade, DJ, 111, 196
Rivera, El, 43
Roland Poet X, 154–157

Sanchez, Sonia, 221–224, 225–227
Shange, Ntozake, 95–97, 98–101
Shannon, Angela, 229
Sherer, Glenis Redmond, 233–234
Shockley, Evelyn E., 64–66
Smith, Patricia, 214–215
Speech, 157–159
Stanard, Christopher, 42
Summer, Cree, 132

Tallie, Mariahadessa "Ekere" 183–185
Taylor, Cheryl Boyce, 126–127
Thompson, Lisa B., 136

Thompson-Cager, Chezia, 208–210
T'Kalla, 206–208
Toney, A. K., 108–109
Touré, Askia M., 202
Troupe, Quincy, 191–195, 216–218

Van Peebles, Mario, 150–151
Vibe, Dr. Madd (a.k.a. The Missin' Link), 16

Walter, Roni, 69–71
War, Michael, 197–199
Ward, Jerry W., Jr., 228
Ward, Pam, 13–14
Warner, Malcolm-Jamal, 133
White-Jackson, Paula, 68
Williams, Crystal A., 170–173
Williams, Karen, 213–214
Williams, Lana C., 212–213
Williams, Marlon C. (PoetX), 205–206
Williams, Niama Leslie, 71–73
Williams, Saul, 237–238
Wilson, A(e)rin, 174–176

Ya Salaam, Kalamu, 227

Derrick I. M. Gilbert (a.k.a. D-Knowledge) is a Ph.D. candidate in Sociology at the University of California, Los Angeles. His essays have appeared in the *National Black Law Journal, Educational Policy, Encyclopedia of African-American Education, Tough Love,* and a variety of other publications. He teaches at UCLA and at Loyola Marymount University. He has appeared in such films as *Higher Learning* and *Panther,* as well as on television shows like the NAACP Image Awards, the *Arsenio Hall Show,* and the *Apollo Comedy Hour.* Derrick has performed with such artists as Me'Shell Ndege'Ocello; Howard Hewitt; Peter Gabriel; Arrested Development; Midnight Oil; Earth, Wind and Fire; and Bill Cosby. He also recorded a poetry/spoken-word CD entitled *All That and a Bag of Words* on Quincy Jones's Qwest Records, and played a lead role on the Rolling Stones' *Voodoo Lounge* CD-ROM. He is currently completing his first volume of poetry and his doctoral dissertation entitled *From Watts to Leimert Park: A Comparative Historical Study of Black Poetry Movements in Los Angeles.*

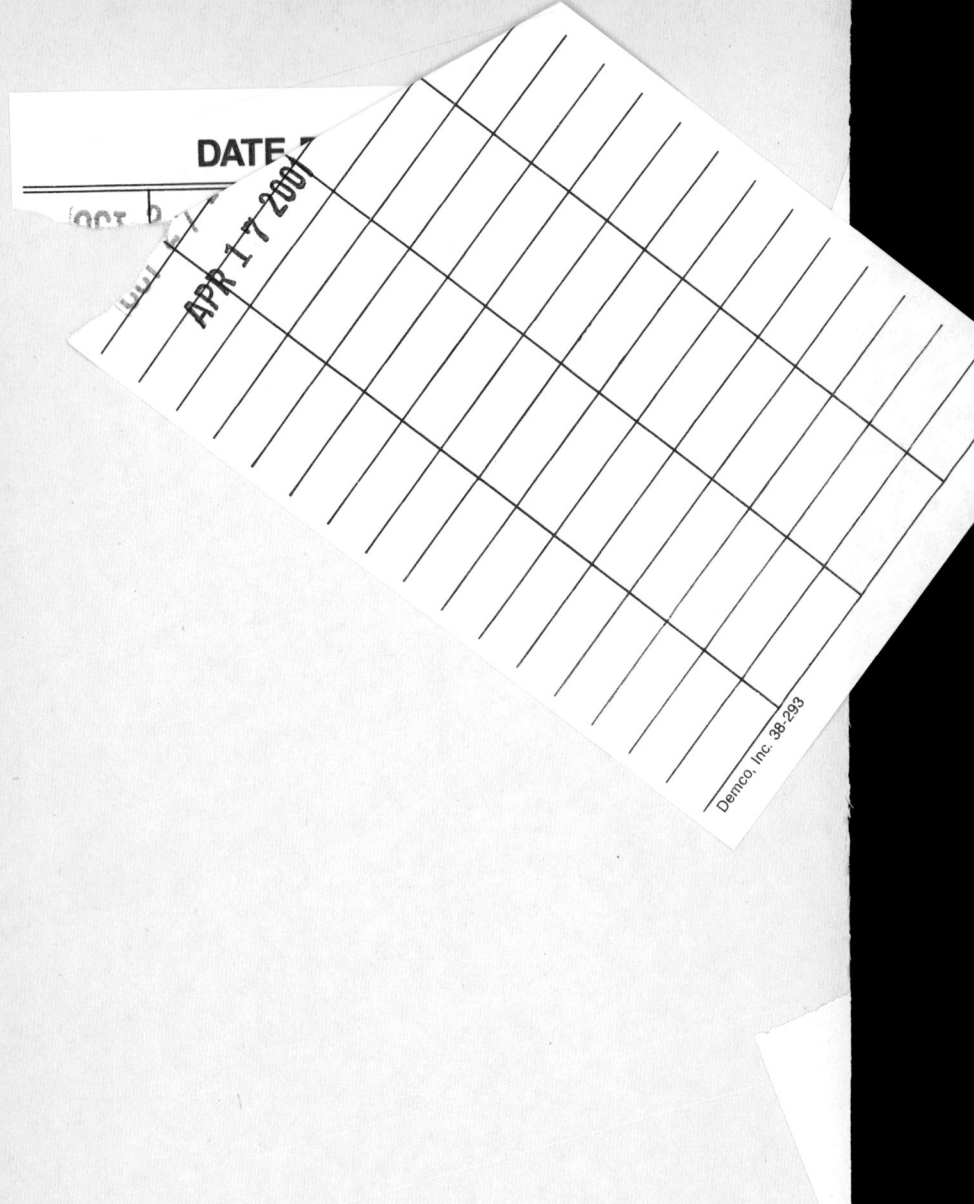